ACQUAINTANCES

With all best wishes

David

SOCIOLOGY *and* **SOCIAL CHANGE**

Series Editors: *Alan* **Warde,** *Nick* **Crossley, University of Manchester**

Published titles

Allison **Cavanagh – Sociology** *in* **the Age** *of* **the Internet**
Amanda **Coffey – Education** *and* **Social Change**
Nick **Crossley – Reflexive Embodiment** *in* **Contemporary Society**
Sara **Delamont – Changing Women, Unchanged Men?**
Andy **Furlong** *and Fred* **Cartmel – Young People** *and* **Social Change (second edition)**
Gail **Hawkes –** *A* **Sociology** *of* **Sex** *and* **Sexuality**
Colin **Hay – Re-stating Social** *and* **Political Change**
Máirtín **Mac an Ghaill – Contemporary Racism** *and* **Ethnicities**
David **Morgan – Acquaintances: The Space Between Intimates** *and* **Strangers**
Mike **Savage – Class Analysis** *and* **Social Transformation**

Acquaintances

The Space Between Intimates *and* Strangers

David **Morgan**

Open University Press

Open University Press
McGraw-Hill Education
McGraw-Hill House
Shoppenhangers Road
Maidenhead
Berkshire
England
SL6 2QL

email: enquiries@openup.co.uk
world wide web: www.openup.co.uk

and Two Penn Plaza, New York, NY 10121–2289, USA

First published 2009

Copyright © David Morgan 2009

All rights reserved. Except for the quotation of short passages for the purposes of criticism and review, no part of this publication may be reproduced, stored in a retrieval system, or transmitted, in any form or by any means, electronic, mechanical, photocopying, recording or otherwise, without the prior permission of the publisher or a licence from the Copyright Licensing Agency Limited. Details of such licences (for reprographic reproduction) may be obtained from the Copyright Licensing Agency Ltd of Saffron House, 6–10 Kirby Street, London, EC1N 8TS.

A catalogue record of this book is available from the British Library

ISBN13: 978 0 335 22160 8 (pb)   978 0 335 22161 5 (hb)
ISBN10: 0 335 22160 2 (pb)   0 335 22161 0 (hb)

Library of Congress Cataloging-in-Publication Data
CIP data applied for

Typeset by RefineCatch Limited, Bungay, Suffolk
Printed in the UK by Bell and Bain Ltd, Glasgow

Mixed Sources
Product group from well-managed forests and other controlled sources
www.fsc.org Cert no. TT-COC-002769
© 1996 Forest Stewardship Council

The *McGraw·Hill* Companies

Contents

Series editors' preface vii
Acknowledgements ix

1 Locating acquaintances 1
Introduction 1
Acquaintanceship: the theoretical tradition 6
Outline 15
A note on method 15
Conclusion 15

2 Acquaintances *in* space: neighbours 18
Introduction 18
Neighbours and neighbouring 20
Neighbourhoods 27
Institutionalized 'neighbours' 30
Conclusion 33

3 'Mates are not friends': acquaintances *and* places *of* work 35
Introduction 35
'Mates are not friends' 36
A case study: 'banana time' 38
The story so far 40
Gender, work and acquaintanceship 41
Other social divisions 45
Changes in work and the development of acquaintances 46
Conclusion 51

4 Relations between professionals *and* clients 53
Introduction 53
Professional themes 55
Professions, professionalization and acquaintanceship:
the consultation 57
Intimacy and distance in professional/client relationships 60

	The consultation: further elaborations	62
	Conclusion	63
5	**Passing acquaintances: overlapping timetables**	65
	Introduction	65
	Rhythms and regularities	67
	Some types of passing acquaintance	69
	Conclusion	74
6	**Fleeting acquaintances *in* time *and* space**	77
	Introduction	77
	Rules of fleeting acquaintances	78
	Knowledge and fleeting acquaintanceship	82
	Contexts and sites	84
	Significance of these encounters	86
	Conclusion	89
7	**Distant *and* unwanted encounters**	91
	Introduction	91
	False friends and unwanted acquaintances	92
	Issues of reciprocity	96
	Disembodied acquaintances	101
	Conclusion	107
8	**Conclusion**	108
	Summary	108
	The practices of acquaintanceship	109
	Sites of acquaintanceship	112
	Significance of acquaintances: for individuals and the self	113
	The social significance of acquaintanceship	115
	Acquaintanceship and everyday life	123
	Final remarks: acquaintanceship and sociological practice	125

References	127
Name index	135
Subject index	137

Series editors' preface

This series is concerned with the critical appraisal of general, substantive theories of social change with reference to different institutional areas of contemporary societies. Each book introduces key current debates and surveys existing sociological argument and research about particular institutional complexes.

This book examines acquaintanceship. David Morgan – a distinguished sociologist of the family, intimacy and masculinity – advances an important and original investigation of the nature of one of the most pervasive, yet under-examined, social relationships in modern urban settings. Somewhere between intimates and strangers, along a continuum stretching from close to distant relationships, acquaintances play a large part in a satisfying and secure everyday life for most of us. Morgan examines acquaintances in the neighbourhood and in the workplace, on the train and in the street. He develops a typology of acquaintanceship which classifies types of contact, contact that we do not necessarily or explicitly value very highly, but which make up largely unavoidable, mostly rewarding, and meaningful connections to other people.

David Morgan uses both classical sociological accounts and the most up-to-date empirical studies to explore its subject matter. It is an exemplary sociological analysis of an important concept concerning the nature of social relationships, social order and the organization of everyday life. It thereby illuminates a phenomenon which has received only fleeting attention in the history of sociology, despite its obvious centrality to personal and social organization. Morgan identifies its key characteristics and explains how it relates to other adjacent, but importantly different, concepts. He both identifies a topic for research and offers a coherent summary of what is currently known about this intriguing subject.

This is a very interesting and challenging book, which will be of great interest to both students and specialist scholars.

Nick Crossley and Alan Warde
University of Manchester
March 2009

Acknowledgements

Numerous people have contributed, directly and indirectly, to the ideas discussed in this book. In some cases they have provided references, made suggestions, asked pertinent questions. In all cases they have provided encouragement and reassurance that this project is interesting and worthwhile. Rather than attempting to list everyone let me indicate some of the sites where I found this support and encouragement.

First, there are my colleagues at the Morgan Centre (where I presented some of these ideas) especially Jennifer Mason and Carol Smart. Next there are my colleagues at Keele University where I have found comments from Ray Pahl, Sue Scott and Pnina Werbner especially helpful. I presented a paper reflecting some of the ideas developed in this book at a meeting organized by the European Sociological Association research network, 'Sociology of Family and Intimate Lives' and held at Lausanne in March 2007. I gained much useful feedback from this presentation and a published version appears in a book edited by E. Widmer, A-M Castren, R. Jallinoja and K. Kaisa and published by Peter Lang.

There are two other important sets of people who provided stimulus. My colleagues at the Norwegian Technological University, Trondheim (NTNU), where I had a visiting professorship for seven years, provided friendship, highly sociable meals and a great deal of encouragement. Further south, in Oslo, I gained a great deal from many stimulating conversations with Halldis Leira. Within the UK, I am continually grateful to my friends and colleagues within the British Sociological Association and its various study groups. Here I would single out for special thanks, other members of the Auto/Biography Study group and, among other individuals within the BSA, Jenny Hockey, Alison James and Sara Edwards.

As on previous occasions, I owe a great debt to my partner, Janet Finch, for many searching questions and a great deal of positive support.

Finally, a thank you to Jack Fray and everyone at Open University Press for their patience and support.

1 Locating acquaintances

Introduction

Acquaintances, as the title of the book suggests, are located in social space. Here, my primary interest is not the physical spaces that people inhabit, the objects and people within them, and the way in which these spaces are invested with human meaning. I am using the term 'social space' to refer to the ways in which individuals are linked to or relate to other individuals, the size and density of these linkages and their overall significance both to the individuals concerned and to the wider social orders within which these are located. 'Social networks' are part of this understanding of social space but are not identical to it. I am also reminded that spatial metaphors such as 'close' or 'distant' are frequently used to describe such relationships.

The basic ideas locating my central concern in this book are simple enough. Any one individual will probably have three sets of people within their social horizons. The closest, more immediate sets of others we describe as intimates: family, friends, lovers. At the outer fringes of this social field there will be strangers, people who are of little or no significance to this individual (except perhaps as imagined threats or objects of charity) and about whom little is known apart from the fact that they are strangers. Between these two, intimates and strangers, lies the subjects of this book: acquaintances. This distinction between intimates, acquaintances and strangers (with 'friends' replacing 'intimates') is found in Adam Smith (1976/1759). Much more recently, Talja Blokland has made a distinction between intimacy, familiarity and anonymous social relations (Blokland 2003: 92–3).

Such a simple mapping may be modified in a variety of ways. First, people may not use this threefold set of distinctions; a more straightforward contrast between 'us' and 'them' (strangers, outsiders) might be sufficient. Second, even where something like this threefold distinction might be used, the size and significance of the individual components might vary considerably. An exploration of wider cultural variations in social mapping is beyond the scope of this present volume. However, if we begin to explore this mapping in the context of, let us say, late modernity we may begin to develop a basis for a wider comparative analysis.

2 Acquaintances

Within late modernity (again, we should not bother too much about terminology at this stage) it would seem that a fair amount is known about intimates and intimacy. Family studies continue to attract a considerable amount of research and this has been joined by studies of sexualities and friendship (Giddens 1992; Jamieson 1998; Smart 2007). We also, probably, know something about strangers, especially about the different ways in which they are constructed, understood, treated and evaluated (Lofland 1973). But little is known, directly, about acquaintances. A brief survey of any library catalogue might support this assertion.

I argue, therefore, that acquaintances lie 'somewhere' between intimates and strangers. In order to identify this 'somewhere' more clearly, we need to have a more exact understanding of 'intimates' and 'strangers'. Intimates can be defined, first, in terms of a range of social relationships which are held to be important to individuals: family, kin, lovers and friends. However, immediately some complexities begin to emerge. For one thing, as a consequence of social or physical distance or some process of estrangement, not all family members might be defined as intimates. Further, although parents and children, friends and lovers may all be defined as intimates they are not intimates in exactly the same way. Indeed, if we take physical sexuality (often popularly identified with intimacy) this may be seen as a requirement for lovers, questionable between friends and strongly prohibited between parents and children or between siblings. Or, to take another widely understood feature of intimacy, the sharing of some of our deepest thoughts, emotions and uncertainties may take place more readily between friends than between family members.

It is possible to see intimacy as consisting of at least three different dimensions, which do not necessarily co-exist in all interpersonal relationships. The first is *physical* or *embodied* intimacy. It is important to stress that this is not simply a question of the physical expression of sexuality. It also includes the physical aspects of caring or tending and those physical signs (holding hands or touching in particular kinds of ways) that demonstrate that some kind of interpersonal bond exists between the two people involved. Goffman (1971) sees these little intimacies as examples of 'tie-signs'.

Second, there is *emotional* intimacy, itself a complex and compound dimension. Thus it can include the sharing of deep feelings, anxieties, doubts and passions. But it can also include the recognition of the emotional needs or likely emotional responses of others, perhaps even at a non verbal level. We may also include here the sharing of interests in music, in work, in the countryside, in politics or in ideas.

Third, there is intimate *knowledge*. Intimates have particular knowledge of each other, knowledge which is conventionally denied to others outside this core of intimacy. Such knowledge may be deployed as a source of amused embarrassment (at wedding speeches for example) or may be the stuff of 'kiss and tell' accounts. We are looking here at the fluid boundaries between the public and the private.

These three dimensions, taken together, pick up most of what is generally understood by the term 'intimacy' and define the characteristics of relationships defined as 'intimate'. One of the virtues of a dimension approach is that it allows for different mixes. Marriage, for example, is assumed (at least in terms of some ideal constructions) to be high on all three dimensions. Parent-child relationships are assumed to have elements of all three (excluding sexual physical intimacy) although emotional intimacy might be more variable, especially over the life course.

Another consequence of this approach is that it can be argued that relationships outside the set of people usually defined as 'intimates' may have some elements of intimacy about them; relationships between professionals and clients for example. This suggests that there is a degree of fuzziness about the boundaries between intimates and acquaintances and this is an issue that will be explored at several points in this book.

Intimates, therefore, occupy one point on the social space within which we locate acquaintances. At the other 'end' we find strangers. Again, however, matters are not straightforward. Most commonly, I suppose, strangers tend to be defined in negative terms, as people who we do not know or recognize. We pass them in the street, stand close to them in the tube or the bus, sit near them in the stadium or the theatre. We recognize certain minimal obligations in turns of not touching, eye contact, avoidance and so on. Social commentators as varied as Engels and Goffman have drawn our attention to the rules strangers observe when passing each other in the street or temporarily sharing the same physical space. These strangers are an integral part of what we understand to be urban life.

But this is not the whole story. Earlier times and other societies suggest that the obligations to strangers sometimes go beyond these minimal interactional expectations. The biblical 'stranger within the gates' and numerous other texts and proverbial expressions indicate that strangers may have a more defined place within the social order and that obligations of hospitality may be extended to such strangers. These are 'known strangers', those who have a definite role within a social situation and whose significance has been discussed by Schutz and Simmel (Schutz 1964; Simmel 1971 [1908]). This 'known' stranger is both near and far, inside and outside. The stranger may be a trader, a regular holiday-maker or an anthropologist.

The difference between the two types of stranger are partly related to the difference between rural and urban, *gemeinschaft* and *gesellschaft*, traditional and modern. Thus 'known strangers' are more likely to be found in smaller, relatively well-bounded communities while 'unknown strangers' are more likely to be a feature of the urban metropolis. The 'known stranger' is contrasted with the members of the community who are the more numerous; the 'unknown stranger' is interchangeable with numerous other 'unknown strangers'. It is clear, therefore, that 'known strangers' might be closer, at least in some respects, to acquaintances and this is how they will be treated in this book. But the boundaries between stranger and non-stranger are fluid and necessarily so.

We can locate acquaintances, therefore, as somewhere 'between' strangers and intimates. We must be careful, however, how we understand this 'between'. Davis (1973: xx) seems to have some kind of hierarchical model, with strangers (and 'role relations') below acquaintances within the non-intimate level and with intimates arranged above the line. He writes of upward

4 Acquaintances

and downward mobility between these levels. This is not what I wish to imply by locating acquaintances as 'between' intimates and strangers. A closer image might be in terms of overlapping circles, with the individual and close intimates at the centre and acquaintances further out. This is a familiar mapping device and probably accords with everyday experience when individuals talk of others as being close or less close. However, it still tends to suggest that acquaintances are on the same scale as these other relationships and hence, necessarily, of lesser significance than intimates. A diagram of overlapping circles might be closer to my intentions. Acquaintances, therefore, are 'somewhere' in between but with no hierarchy of relationships being implied.

We have, therefore, some approximate kind of mapping of acquaintances in a wider spectrum of social relationships. But this is still rather negative. Acquaintances are not intimates and they are not strangers; but is it possible to say something more positive than this?

The first point to make is that acquaintances have some of the characteristics of intimates already outlined. To illustrate this let me provide an everyday narrative. I leave my house one morning and see a neighbour returning from walking the dog. We exchange a few words and I continue to walk to the doctor's surgery. There I have a short wait before I see my GP. In the waiting room I see a former colleague, now retired and we have a brief chat before he is called. I discuss my relatively minor complaint with my GP and she asks me about other members of my family. On the way home I stop off at a corner shop, exchange some light-hearted chat with the owner and a couple of the other customers and return home.

We may see here little fragments of intimacy. These include verbal exchanges, mutual recognition, knowledge of or by the other and, in the case of the GP, some slight physical intimacy as she takes my blood pressure. These are echoes of other intimacies, perhaps, although they go so far and no further. For example, my neighbour knows who I am and who I live with, has some idea when I am away or on holiday, knows how I keep my garden and when I am entertaining friends. I have similar overlapping knowledge of my neighbour and his social circle. Yet, I probably would not call my neighbour an intimate; if he were I should probably use some other term such as 'friend'.

Note here, a slight shift in emphasis. Acquaintances are defined not so much as people who are not intimates but as people with whom there are some slight echoes or fragments of intimacy. Some of these are reciprocated, others are not. Some of these exchanges have a basis of equality while others, again, do not have such a basis or premise. Many of these everyday exchanges are commonplace, barely worth mentioning. Yet it would be difficult to describe or account for social life without them.

There are also overlaps between acquaintances and strangers. Acquaintances are different from both the known and the unknown strangers. But they have something of the stranger about them and that is a measure of distance. I have only been into my neighbour's house on a few occasions and all of these have been social events with several other people. On these occasions my visits have been confined to one or two rooms or possibly the garden. My GP's interest in the other members of my family is, to a very large extent, a professional one. The exchanges in the corner shop rarely go beyond everyday chat and joking. And in all of these examples, and others, there seems to be some kind of unwritten pact that says this is how we want it. Again, therefore, it is not simply that acquaintances are not strangers; they also have something in common with strangers and that can be defined, for the present, as a measure of social distance.

There are some further points that may be made about this analysis. The first is, to repeat a point made earlier, that the boundaries are very fuzzy, especially when we take the passing of time into account. Strangers can become acquaintances and acquaintances can become intimates and the reverse processes are also possible. Nevertheless, at a single point of time, we can map our social world into strangers, acquaintances and intimates.

Second, it always has to be remembered that there are cultural variations and the 'rules' or unwritten pacts will vary between societies and within societies. Guide- books and etiquette books go to some length to provide advice as to how to negotiate these different relationships. Thus in some guidance on 'French Etiquette' the reader is told: 'DO acknowledge your immediate co-travellers on a plane or in a train but don't feel obliged to get into conversation. A simple *bonjour* will do' (*France*, August 2005: P7). In general, it may be said that a large part of this guidance is to do with understanding the proper balance between intimacy and distance. Although the precise parameters might vary, the notion of some kind of balance provides a common thread. It should also be stated, for the sake of completeness, that there will always be some individual variation. Thus, some people may be described as 'keeping themselves to themselves' or being 'over-familiar' and clearly societies and social situations differ according to the amount of variation that is permitted before sanctions are applied.

There is one further feature of some importance when we come to defining acquaintances. This is the lack of interchangeability (Blokland 2003: 73). Even where our knowledge of neighbours, professionals, people we meet in the street, workmates or colleagues is quite limited they are not interchangeable. The woman who runs the corner shop is not simply to be defined in terms of interchangeable categories such as gender, ethnicity or age. It is *this* woman, with a distinctive voice, physical appearance, mode of dress and so on in *this* particular shop, with all its distinctive ways of displaying the goods for sale. This shows some points of overlap with both intimates and strangers. Intimates are never interchangeable. Strangers, say in a crowd, may frequently be so but one stranger can easily stand out in some way and make a shift in the direction of acquaintanceship.

Thus, to sum up so far, acquaintances are not simply understood in negative terms as being not intimates and not strangers. They are not interchangeable. Rather we can say more positively that they are characterized by a particular mix of intimacy and distance, although the intimacy is rarely very great and the distance rarely consequential. But this does not take us much further. Or is, perhaps, the very vagueness of the social terrain an inherent part of our definition or understanding of acquaintanceship?

Acquaintanceship: the theoretical tradition

A conventional literature survey would be out of place here, if only for the reason that there is little in the way of direct literature. Look up the word 'acquaintance' in any library catalogue or sociological reference book. Nevertheless, it is possible to find some passing references, and sometimes more, to acquaintanceship within the theoretical literature and, further, it is possible to extrapolate from particular texts in order to develop and provide some solidity to the idea of acquaintanceship. In what follows, I refer heavily to some of Simmel and Goffman's writings, two writers who, in different ways, were concerned with the forms and the practices of interpersonal relationships within modern society, a field which includes, but is clearly, not limited to acquaintances. I have also found some stimulus in the writings of Elias, Schutz, Sartre and Merton. However, I shall not deal with these sources individually but instead I shall highlight some themes that seem to emerge from this exploration of the theoretical literature.

But I begin with Adam Smith. Having developed my threefold distinction between intimates, acquaintances and strangers, I was intrigued to find that Adam Smith had a somewhat similar set of distinctions:

> We expect less sympathy from a common acquaintance than from a friend: we cannot open to the former all those little circumstances which we can unfold to the latter: we assume, therefore, more tranquillity before him, and endeavour to fix our thoughts upon those general outlines of our situation which he is willing to consider. We expect still less sympathy from an assembly of strangers, and we assume, therefore, still more tranquillity before them, and always endeavour to bring down our passion to that pitch, which the particular company we are in may be expected to go along with. Nor is this only an assumed appearance: for if we are at all masters of ourselves, the presence of a mere acquaintance will really compose us, still more than that of a friend: and that of an assembly of strangers still more than that of an acquaintance.
>
> (Adam Smith 1976/1759)

This is a remarkable passage in many ways. For our present purposes, it raises several themes to which we shall return at various stages in this exploration. First, Smith presents some kind of differentiation between 'friends', 'acquaintances' and 'strangers'. Second, there is some suggestion, in the references to a 'common' or a 'mere' acquaintance, that these exist in terms of some kind of hierarchy. However, there is also the suggestion that acquaintanceship might have some more positive features, indicated in the way in which individuals compose themselves or assume more tranquillity in the presence of the other. Perhaps it is not a hierarchy after all?

It is clearly an interactionist approach that is being proposed; he is concerned with the space between a self and others. Further, to continue to use more modern terminology, selves are constructed through these interactions with strangers and acquaintances such that our adjustments in the face of the other are not simply assumed, like a mask, but are incorporated into our identities.

A hierarchy of relationships?

Adam Smith is certainly aware of some kind of hierarchy in which acquaintances are above strangers but below friends even if he does not necessarily endorse such an evaluation. Numerous examples from everyday speech would seem to endorse this distinction and this is reflected in some writings on intimate relationships, for example as we have seen, M.S. Davis (1973).

Simmel's writings would seem to support this ranking when he describes acquaintances as 'sociologically highly peculiar' relationships (Wolff 1950: 320). Such relationships contrast with those 'rooted in the total personality' and, unlike these more rounded relationships, involve 'no actual insight into the individual nature of the personality'. When we respond to an acquaintance, we simply respond to that aspect of the other which is presented to the outside world not to 'what is essential in him'. However, with Simmel, nothing is quite so straightforward as we shall see.

Nevertheless, this kind of contrast would seem to be very deeply rooted in current understandings of intimacy. On the one side we find instrumentality and superficiality; on the other mutuality and authenticity. It would seem that as intimate relationships become more and more valued, so the hierarchical contrast between acquaintances and intimates grows. However, the literature suggests a more complex picture.

The blurring of the boundaries

Although, in the earlier passage, Adam Smith seems to be clear about the boundaries between friends and acquaintances, other eighteenth-century figures, Samuel Johnson for example, seem to have used the terms interchangeably. And indeed, elsewhere in his book on moral sentiments, the distinctions are not quite as clear as they might at first have seemed. He notes that 'colleagues in offices, partners in trade, call one another brothers, and frequently feel towards one another as if they really were so' (1976/1759: 223–4). If this is the case, where then is the boundary between friends and acquaintances to be drawn?

In Simmel's writings, we can find a range of direct and indirect references to the idea of acquaintanceship although the overall picture becomes somewhat more blurred. In his well-known essay on 'The Metropolis and Mental Life', although he does not appear to use the word directly, he repeats the contrast between intimates and others already mentioned. The contrast here is between the emotional relationships based upon individuality and the more intellectual relationships associated with the development of the money economy. His illustrations refer to 'his merchant, his customer, and with his servant, and frequently with the persons with whom he is thrown into obligatory association' (Simmel [1903]1971: 326–7). It may not escape notice that these others are similar, in some respects, to those whom Adam Smith describes as calling each other brothers. These are certainly not strangers and

8 Acquaintances

could almost certainly be described as acquaintances. Relations with such individuals might be characterized as fleeting and superficial but this is by no means inevitably the case. Indeed, if the encounters with these others are repeated, as must often be the case, it seems unlikely that they will remain at a purely instrumental level. It certainly seems likely that Simmel is overstating the contrast and that his writing here is part of a well established negative construction of the modern metropolis.

Elsewhere in his writings, Simmel's 'social circles' (about which more later) could include both intimates and acquaintances. His example of 'the republic of scholars' would certainly suggest this. At the other end of the continuum, his 'stranger' – not 'the wanderer who comes today and goes tomorrow' but 'the man who comes today and stays tomorrow' is a 'known stranger' and almost certainly, therefore, a kind of acquaintance (Simmel 1971[1908]: 143). Although Simmel appears to have relatively few direct references to acquaintances, the idea of acquaintanceship seems to pervade much of his writings.

Similar ambiguities appear in the writings of Goffman. Taking these as a whole it would seem that he is concerned with relationships of all kinds, from intimates to strangers. However, when he is concerned with intimates he is more concerned with the way in which partners 'do intimacy' in public rather than with the actual content of that intimacy. Generally speaking, what takes place between actors (especially in public places) is of greater importance than the content or meaning of such relationships.

There is a brief reference to 'acquaintanceship' at the end of his address on *The Interaction Order* (Goffman 1983) where he supplies his preferred term 'knowership'. This shift in terminology is, as we shall see, significant. In the discussion that follows he moves back and forth across the boundary between acquaintances and intimates, showing his main concern to be those who have obligations to exchange not merely greetings but also bits of their biographies. These he distinguishes from 'mere acquaintanceship'.

More specific references to acquaintances appear in *Behaviour in Public Places* (1963) where he analyses focussed interaction. Acquaintances have the right to initiate face engagements and there is not only cognitive recognition but also social recognition as well. In other words, I do not simply register that this other person is a neighbour or a colleague but I also express this recognition through my words and bodily demeanour. However, here he devotes 11 pages to acquaintances and 23 pages to engagements between the 'un-acquainted' (although the very process of engagement presumably leads to some sense of acquaintanceship?) and it is clear where his interests lie in this particular text.

Closer to intimacy, in his *Relations in Public* (1971) there are overlaps between acquaintanceship and 'anchored relationships', which are contrasted with anonymous relationships. These anchored relationships have a 'career or a natural development' and hence could apply to relationships between acquaintances. However, it is clear in this context that he is more interested in intimate relationships and the use of tie signs to demonstrate that such a relationship exists. While Goffman is certainly interested in acquaintances he is less interested in formulating the differences between different kinds of relationships and more interested in the interaction processes themselves.

To take one further example from the literature, Granovetter (1973) argues that the strength of a tie between individuals can be based upon four dimensions: the amount of time that the participants devote to each other; the emotional intensity; intimacy (which is equated with mutual confiding) and the existence, degree and kind of reciprocal services. On this basis ties can be described as 'strong', 'weak' or 'absent'. With such a multidimensional approach, the lines between intimates and acquaintances necessarily become blurred. Depending on the dimension chosen, ties between family members could be weak while those between neighbours could be strong. It is interesting, however, that he gives 'nodding acquaintance' as an example of an absent tie. What is perhaps missing here is some sense of the knowledge that actors have of others.

Writings on acquaintanceship are, as I have said, relatively few. Where writers have dealt with acquaintanceship to some degree, the general impression would seem to be that this is not their first concern and that the boundaries between acquaintanceship and other kinds of relationships would seem to be blurred. This should be expected. If individuals refer to 'friends' in all sorts of different ways it should not be surprising that understandings of acquaintances are often equally indistinct and that usages vary between social circles and over time. Further, it is reasonable to suppose, as Goffman reminds us, that relationships have a career and that, over time, acquaintances can sometimes become intimates. It seems prudent, therefore, to accept that the boundaries between acquaintances and others are blurred. What is of interest is the range of issues involved. These include the idea of acquaintanceship as a form of knowledge and the suggestion that its significance might have changed over historical time.

A form of knowledge

Acquaintanceship can be stated to be a form of knowledge about the other. This understanding is in line with common usages of the word 'acquaintance', where some kind of knowledge, not necessarily of other people, is implied: 'I have been one acquainted with the night' (Robert Frost 1928/1951). As this quotation implies, such knowledge may not simply be cognitive, but it may have some emotional dimensions also.

Simmel recognizes that knowledge is involved but feels that it is a rather inferior or second-rate knowledge. Initially, he limits the knowledge to the kind that occurs in an introduction, simply taking account of the other's existence: 'acquaintance depends upon the knowledge of the *that* of the personality, not of its *what*' (Wolff 1950: 320, original emphasis). However, it could be argued that the acquaintanceship implied in Simmel's discussion of the stranger – in our terms a 'known stranger' – suggests something more than this. Similarly, his celebrated discussion of 'pure sociability' (which could be seen as a core activity between acquaintances and intimates) suggests practices of deeper significance both for the individuals concerned and for the wider social order. To recognize another as a witty conversationalist or an accomplished flirt is to begin to have a knowledge which goes beyond formal introductions.

10 Acquaintances

Goffman, in his turn, stresses knowledge and provides a more positive slant to it. In his discussion of 'anchored relationships' he almost provides a definition of acquaintanceship: 'a framework of mutual knowing, which retains, organizes, and applies the experience the ends have of one another' (1971: 189). A more pithy, but insightful, definition may be found in the following: 'a state of mutually admitted mutual knowing' (Goffman 1971: 205). On the other hand, a more extended version of this might be found in the earlier, *Behaviour in Public Places*: 'Its preconditions are satisfied when each of two individuals can personally identify the other by knowledge that distinguishes this one from everyone else and when each acknowledges to the other that this state of mutual information exists' (Goffman 1963: 112). In this context it is probably more accurate to recognize that Goffman is talking about more intimate relationships. However, such relationships have a career and may well begin with acquaintance. The question of mutuality needs to be explored further but Goffman makes one interesting point about acquaintanceship, namely its non-reversability. We may fall out of love or cease to be friends but one can 'never resort to non-acquaintanceship'.

As we have seen, Goffman highlights the processual nature of acquaintanceship, a point also stressed by the social psychologist, Newcomb: 'In almost any face-to-face encounter of two or more human beings, processes occur that are acquaintance-like' (Newcomb 1961: 259). It might also be suggested that Homan's discussion about the relationships between interaction and liking also includes this processual and temporal dimension (Homans 1951).

Yet Goffman seems to go further and talks of obligations as well as of processes:

> In sum, then, whenever we come into contact with another through the mail, over the telephone, in face-to-face talk, or even merely through immediate co-presence, we find ourselves with one central obligation: to render our behaviour understandably relevant to what the other can come to perceive is going on.
> (in Lemert and Branaman 1997: 192)

Again, such an account does not clearly distinguish between intimates and acquaintances (or, indeed, strangers) although it could be argued that the fulfilling of such an obligation is, at the very least, the beginning of acquaintanceship.

It is important to distinguish between two sorts of knowledge. The first is the more explicit or overt knowledge that individuals provide for each other in the course of a conversation (say, at a dinner party) or over a series of conversations. However, in addition, there is also the sort of knowledge that is given off by the other, even where no verbal interaction takes place. We come to know (or sometimes to assume we know) a great deal about another individual through their physical appearance and mode of dress, their embodied ways of being in the world, the tone of their voice and so on. These non-verbal aspects of everyday knowledge are as much part of what I understand by the term 'acquaintanceship' as are the more overt exchanges of biographical information discussed by Goffman.

One further and related question, implied in much of what has gone before, is whether an essential part of the knowledge that acquaintances possess of each other should include the name of the other. Names and naming are complex matters and provide valuable clues to everyday interactional processes. Whether we use a formal mode of address, a first name or a nickname requires detailed social understanding and skill. The ability to provide and to use a name of and for the other clearly distinguishes an acquaintance from a stranger although I would not wish to see this ability as an essential defining characteristic of acquaintanceship. Let it be said, for the time being, that with acquaintanceship there is always the possibility of finding out the name of the other. I may not know the name of the person who regularly passes me on the street but there is a good chance that I might discover this if I wish to do so.

What this suggests is that one feature of this knowledge between acquaintances is that we are not necessarily or even usually dealing with a single dyadic relationship but with non-dyadic relationships or, more exactly, a series of dyads. Acquaintanceship in this sense may be seen as a form of bricolage. The idea of serial acquaintanceship is something to which we shall return.

To sum up so far: acquaintanceship is a form of knowledge of the other. It is a process and, arguably, involves some mutual obligations. The degree and kind of mutuality or reciprocity has yet to be determined.

Intimacy and distance

The knowledge at the heart of acquaintanceship is clearly distinct from the merely categorical knowledge that may inform two strangers who pass each other in the street. It is also distinct from the complex and multi-stranded knowledges that link intimates. In commonsensical terms, as Frisby notes, 'it would be possible to grade all social interactions on a scale of proximity or distance' (Frisby 1992: 106). Similarly, Elias's discussion of involvement and detachment, is also relevant here (Elias 1987). However, the idea of a scale or a continuum might understate possible qualitative differences in the comparison between intimates and acquaintances. Distance, detachment and holding back may be questioned in intimate relations; they may almost be required between acquaintances.

This is certainly implied in the quotation from Adam Smith with which I began. It is also argued by Simmel as I have already indicated and demonstrated most clearly in his discussion of pure sociability as a play form of sociation. Sociability is based upon conversation where the obligation is less to be found in the topics of the conversation but far more in the maintenance of the conversation in a way which is mutually agreeable. Simmel's discussion of 'coquetry' or flirtation perfectly captures this sense of a fine balance between intimacy and distance. This sense of a skilful balance is also conveyed when Simmel argues that acquaintanceship is the proper seat of discretion (Wolff 1950: 320). In his terms, 'what is not concealed may be known, what is not revealed must not be known' (p. 321). Further links may be made to ideas of honour and personal space, themes that are also very much at the heart of many of Goffman's writings.

We shall find several examples of this idea of a balance between intimacy and distance in the chapters that follow. We find it in discussions of relationships between professionals and clients, in accounts of relationships between colleagues and co-workers and in discussions of neighbourhoods and neighbouring. Despite the fact that words like 'reserve' and 'distance' frequently have negative connotations, I wish to stress the more positive features of these balances. Acquaintances are not to be judged as falling short of some ideal standard set by intimacy.

Acquaintances and networks

We may have a handful of intimates but many acquaintances. Some of these acquaintances may be known to each other (or to other intimates) while others may not. This 'spatial organization of the life-world' (Schutz and Luckmann 1973: 41) is at the heart of network analysis as it is central to Elias's 'figurational sociology' (Elias 1970). When Bendix translated what might have been more accurately rendered as 'overlapping social circles' as 'the web of group affiliations' he may have provided a misleading sense of concreteness to Simmel's analysis, certainly in the use of 'group' if less so in the use of 'web' (Simmel 1955). Certainly, what we are concerned with in thinking about acquaintances in the plural is less a set of group affiliations and more a series of ties, the only common feature of which, in many cases, is their link to ego.

Whether the term 'social network' is appropriate in the face of such potentially loose-knit sets of ties is a moot point. Notions of 'seriality' (to use Sartre's term; Craib 1976) or 'bricolage' may be more to the point, especially where time is taken into consideration. However, network analysis as it has developed has usefully reminded us of themes of degrees of interconnectedness and the possible overlaps between intimates and acquaintances as well as providing some valuable tools for the comparative analysis of sets of social relations. It seems advisable, therefore, to continue to refer to social networks in relation to acquaintances while retaining an awareness that this approach may sometimes limit our understanding.

The positive value of acquaintance

I hope that I have said enough to indicate that acquaintanceship is more than a residual relationship. It should be studied in its own right and according to its own logic. We may see, following Simmel, the ever widening sets of others to whom we are connected – on whatever basis – as a sign of the development of human culture. We may see, as Adam Smith suggests, some positive value in the lowering of the passions that takes place as we move from friends to acquaintances. We may positively value the processes of bricolage through which, in Weinstein and Weinstein's striking words, we 'construct a self and a strategy of living from the shards of objective culture' (1991: 167).

Equally, and following Granovetter, we may recognize and explore the 'strength of weak ties' (1973). Weak ties, he argues, are more important in terms of their bridging rather than their bonding characteristics: 'those to whom we are weakly tied are more likely to move in circles different from our own and will thus have access to information different from that which we receive' (1973: 1371). The 'small world' phenomenon is more likely to be a product of acquaintanceship rather than of intimacies, of weak rather than of strong ties.

There are a variety of ways, therefore, in which acquaintances may have their own significance. This may be true whether we are thinking about individuals, about particular social institutions or sets of practices (communities, places of work) or whether we are talking at a more general societal level. These will be explored in some details in subsequent chapters and in the conclusion.

Acquaintanceship in history

Although the term 'acquaintance' might be relatively new it is likely that the sense of others located somewhere between intimates and strangers has a longer history. From one angle it might almost seem to be a question of mathematics. We may assume that there are limits, practical and psychological, to the number of intimates that we have although this will vary according to individual personality and social circumstances. Strangers, on the other hand, have always been with us although their significance and how they are treated will, similarly, to subject to considerable variation. Thus there will always be some people who are not exactly intimates and not exactly strangers and to whom we may designate the term 'acquaintance'.

This does not say very much but does help us to frame the following questions. Is it possible to talk about a history, or histories, of acquaintanceship? And, more specifically, have acquaintances become more or less important in late modern society?

Simmel's rather dismissive discussion of acquaintanceship suggests that the idea, at least, is relatively recent and socially limited: 'Aside from interest groups but aside, equally, from relationships rooted in the total personality, there is the sociologically highly peculiar relationship which, in our times, among educated strata, is designated simply as "acquaintance"' (Wolff 1950: 320). There may be issues of translation here; as we have seen the term 'acquaintance' was used by Adam Smith. Nevertheless, it also seems to be the case that there was considerable flexibility in the use of the term 'acquaintance' in the eighteenth century and its usage may overlap considerable with that of 'friend' (Tadmor 2001). Yet, even allowing for the fact that Simmel here seems to be taking a rather restricted notion of acquaintance (do not interest groups include acquaintances?) there is some suggestion that the term is of relatively recent origin.

Indirectly, we may find support for this argument in some of Simmel's other writings. His discussion of the development of group affiliations (or social circles) links this to a wider process of historical and cultural change: 'The number of different social groups in which the individual participates is one of the earmarks of culture' (1955: 138). These developments are also linked to what later sociologists might identify as a process of 'individualization': 'the fact of multiple group-participation creates in turn a new subjective element' (p. 141).

It would therefore to be a reasonable extrapolation from Simmel's writings to argue that, as human societies move away from being dominated by more 'natural' groups, so we find a greater proportion of acquaintances in our sets of others. This evolutionary approach, whereby the proportion of 'acquaintances' becomes larger, would seem to be found in several passages from his writings.

A somewhat different picture might be found in his essay on 'The metropolis and mental life' where the contrast is that between emotional relationships based upon individuality and the more abstract relationships, characteristic of a money economy. Yet does not the advanced division of labour that is said to characterize modern cities also allow for the development of acquaintances, people about whom our knowledge is partial but who, as a consequence of their singularity, can scarcely be classified as strangers? (A barber, an owner of an antiquarian bookshop, a chiropractor?)

In the writings of Elias, it is possible again through some extrapolation to see some link between his idea of the civilizing process and the development of acquaintanceship. Mennell and Goudsblom describe what might be seen as the conditions for the development of acquaintanceship: 'more people are forced more often to pay more attention to more people, in more varied circumstances' (1998: 18). We might, however, quibble about the use of the word 'forced'.

Elias's account of the consequences of these developments has strong echoes of Adam Smith: 'The individual is compelled to regulate his conduct in an increasingly differentiated, more even and more stable manner' (Elias 1998: 52). Elsewhere, Elias writes of the changes in the 'We/I' balance and claims that, by the late twentieth century, society had almost reached the stage of the 'We-less I' (Elias 1991). Again it is not difficult to see an anticipation of subsequent discussions of individualization. Where 'we' relationships continue to exist they suffer from greater impermanence. This would seem to suggest a contrast between a severely truncated set of intimate relations or solidarities and a world of relative strangers. When Elias writes of 'we-relationships' he is referring to 'family, domicile or native region and affiliation to a nation state' (1991: 202).

However, there can be several 'we's, reflecting the multiple and complex range of usages of this simple word. 'We' can refer to the kinds of social solidarities that Elias seems to have in mind here. But 'we' can also simply refer to two or more people engaged in some kind of common (however short-lived) set of practices. Thus: 'we met for coffee', 'we shared a taxi', 'we are near neighbours'. It is likely that the decline of 'we' relationships in Elias's use of the term are not replaced simply by greater individualization but by the development of more serialised acquaintances, different kinds of we relationships.

I shall return to a discussion of the significance of acquaintanceship in late modern society in my concluding chapter. However it may be suggested that the whole drift of sociological analysis, more or less from its earliest days, would suggest the growth of conditions favourable to the development of acquaintanceship. These would include the familiar themes of the development of capitalism and a market economy, urbanization, industrialization, geographical and social mobility and so on. At the same time there has been a development of the use of the term 'acquaintance' and that changes in these usages parallel these wider social changes.

Outline

This book begins with the relatively familiar and moves out to the less familiar. Chapter 2 deals with acquaintances in space, that is relationships between neighbours and within neighbourhoods. Chapter 3 deals with another rich source of acquaintanceship, that is places of work. Chapter 4 continues this to some extent, while opening up new issues in a consideration of professional-client relationships. Chapter 5 looks at passing acquaintances, the acquaintances that arise out of overlapping timetables in modern society. Chapter 6 deals with fleeting acquaintances arising out of brief overlaps in terms of time and space and frequently centrally to do with leisure and urban living. Chapter 7 takes up three topics that have been somewhat underplayed in previous chapters: unwelcome acquaintances, questions of reciprocity or non-reciprocity and questions of embodiment. In the conclusion, I attempt to assess the overall significance of this exploration for individuals, for society and for social enquiry.

A note on method

This book is not based, except sometimes indirectly, on systematic empirical research. To ask for evidence of such research would be to misunderstand the nature of this project which is to open up a relatively novel area of social enquiry. My hope is that it may stimulate such research or that it might provide a framework for the reinterpretation of existing data.

I have already said that there is not a great deal in the literature that is directly about acquaintanceship. Therefore, a great deal of this discussion is based upon existing published work designed to explore other issues. The selection of texts is necessarily somewhat haphazard, based often on works I remember reading in the past, perhaps for teaching or for other writings or works which might seem promising in exploring such specific topics as neighbourhoods or work and employment. The result is fairly wide ranging, snatching ideas from studies of communities and workplaces, urban sociology and literature on professionalization. I have augmented such reading with references from novels or films and from my own autobiography. The test of the success or otherwise of this enterprise is less to do with reliability and validity and more to do with the extent to which it initiates further enquiries.

In other words, all this is a form of bricolage. Rather like acquaintanceship itself.

Conclusion

The main points to emerge from the discussion so far are as follows:
- Acquaintanceship is a topic worthy of investigation.
- There is considerable uncertainty about how it is to be defined and the ways in which it might be distinguished from intimate relations on the one hand and encounters with strangers on the other.
- There is also considerable variation in the use of the term, ranging from

16 Acquaintances

situations where the term is hardly ever used to ones where the term is frequently used and with a clear sense of distinction from other kinds of social relationships.
- Acquaintanceship deals with a form of knowledge, one that is distinct from the categorical knowledge that defines meetings between strangers and the detailed and personal knowledge that obtains between intimates.
- Acquaintanceship is more than a residual category and can be seen much more positively. To adopt a different language, it can be seen as performing important functions for individuals and social institutions.
- It is likely that the nature and significance of acquaintanceship has changed over time and probably also varies between and within different societies.

It can be seen that we are left with what is potentially a very large area in the space between intimates and strangers. We are dealing with workmates and colleagues, neighbours, people we pass in the street on a regular basis, professional/client relationships, and possibly relationships with celebrities or even fictional characters. We either need to narrow the field considerably or to make some provision for distinctions within it.

As a preliminary way of ordering the discussion, I suggest that we consider the intersection of two continua:

A In terms of knowledge: very simply, this can run from high to low, the only limitation being that the knowledge must be more than the mere categorical. Even so, this may be quite limited: 'The woman who lives at number 23', for example. Yet, even here, the person so defined is not interchangeable with any other person.

B In terms of contact: at a first attempt, I opt for the simplicity of frequency of contact, recognising that we cannot read quality off from quantity. This can be seen as ranging from zero to high.

For obvious reasons, it seems sensible to see the intersection of these two continua as producing an open space rather than the more familiar four boxes:

1 A combination of a high degree of contact with high levels of knowledge. This is close to what Goffman means by 'knowership'. Some degree of reciprocity is assumed and those in this space are distinct from intimates although may become so in the future. Examples here include some (but not all) neighbours, and some, but not all, workmates, colleagues and co-participants in voluntary associations.
2 A high degree of knowledge, combined with little or no actual contact. Clearly, also, there is little or no reciprocity here. Examples here could include celebrities and fictional characters and possibly also people at the top of organizational hierarchies.
3 A reasonably high degree of contact but with relatively little knowledge. Some small amount of reciprocity may be assumed. These are the *passing acquaintances*, the people one might pass or see on a fairly regular basis.
4 Low contact combined with low knowledge. This is clearly at the other end of the scale, close to strangers. But there is some non-categorical

knowledge and some modest reciprocity. Examples of these *fleeting acquaintances* may be taxi drivers, shop assistants and other members of the service economy.

I shall pursue these distinctions in the chapters to come. For the time being, let us conclude with Simmel's memorable phrase: 'the delicate invisible threads that are woven between one person and another' (quoted in Frisby 1992: 14). These are delicate because they often consist of a single strand or because they do not persist outside a particular spatial/temporal framework except in memory. They are invisible, because they frequently go unrecognized. They are woven, because they exist within a temporal stream, have a history and require some work to develop and to sustain them.

2 Acquaintances *in* space: neighbours

Introduction

In Alfred Hitchcock's film, *Rear Window*, a successful press photographer is confined to his apartment as a result of a broken leg. In the heat of the summer, sounds from other apartments drift over to him. From his vantage point he can get fleeting and partial insights into the lives of his neighbours. He has the opportunity to construct stories about them. There is the young composer, hoping to make the big time. There is 'Miss Lonelyhearts', always hoping for a gentleman to call. And there is the man who may or may not be in the process of murdering his wife. All that we know about these neighbours is what we, and the central protagonist, are allowed to see. The people in this apartment block are neighbours in that they share space but they do not, as far as we know, engage in neighbouring. Yet they have some knowledge of each other and this knowledge is sometimes intimate knowledge.

When people make critiques of the loneliness and alienation of urban life they may be operating with this kind of image in mind. People live in relatively close proximity to each other and, to this extent, know something about one another, but cannot be said in any other sense to share lives. These tendencies are exacerbated by high rates of geographical mobility, different working hours and practices and demographic trends.

However, there are many different kinds of neighbourhoods and forms of urban living and not all of them conform to this particular model. Communities may be found within cities or parts of cities. There may, as Frankenberg (1966) argues qualitative changes as we move from the rural to the less rural but there may still be some warrant for the use of the term 'community'. Even in these more anonymous or fragmented residential areas, the people we live close to are not complete strangers. They are often more like 'known strangers' in that we do have some knowledge about them even if we rarely do anything more jointly than exchange formal greetings.

In this chapter, I aim to explore how our living arrangements, where we live, shapes our acquaintances. Where we live may also include more tightly structured forms of living arrangements such as billeting in the army, dormitories in schools, prison or hospital accommodation and so on, mostly, therefore in those kinds of situations described by Goffman as 'total institutions' (Goffman 1968 [1961]). I shall pay some attention to these organizations while concentrating on household-based arrangements. For the most part these other organizational forms, total institutions, may be relatively short-term living arrangements with a considerable amount of turnover. Nevertheless they have a significance in the lives of a large section of the population and hence can be linked to the theme of acquaintanceship.

Living arrangements may, of course, include intimates as well as acquaintances. Indeed more traditional understandings of 'community' will concentrate on networks of family, kin and friends rather than acquaintances who may either be ignored or subsumed within the more general idea of community. Again, my concern here is with those others who tend to be marginalized or ignored within the community study tradition but who may, in different ways, contribute to a sense of community living.

I need to provide some working definitions here. In talking about 'neighbourhood' I am talking about a locality which has some kind of meaning for the participants. This locality may be large or small, weakly bounded or strongly bounded. It may correspond to official or administrative boundaries or it may overlap with or be included within such boundaries. It may be relatively heterogeneous or homogeneous. Perceptions of neighbourhood boundaries and core characteristics may differ between individuals included within a neighbourhood.

Neighbours are those who live close to you in a neighbourhood but the sum total of neighbours might be less than the number of persons occupying a neighbourhood. Neighbours need not be confined to those living immediately next door but probably do not extend much beyond although, again, the range can be very fluid. Neighbours might be evaluated as good or bad and while there might be some overlap between these ideas and ideas of good and bad neighbourhoods, the two are not the same.

Neighbouring refers to a set of practices that can be associated with neighbours and is generally a positive term. It might include, for example, a willingness to carry out some chores for each other or adopting a general watchfulness on behalf of the other. Watering plants, feeding domestic animals or generally keeping an eye open for strangers when the neighbour is away might be among these positively evaluated neighbouring practices. But expectations of good neighbours need not necessarily include such neighbouring practices; you can have neighbours, even good neighbours, without neighbouring.

The reasons for this apparent paradox lie in the fact that discussions about the evaluation of neighbours revolve around some kind of continuum from involvement to detachment or between closeness and distance. Good neighbours may be helpful, willing to run little errands, watchful for your interests and generally friendly. But good neighbours may also keep themselves to themselves, not want to know your business, maintain a friendly but respectful detachment. Bad neighbours may be over-detached, unfriendly and snooty. But they may also be over intrusive, nosey and overfamiliar.

This leads to some knotty personal and sociological problems. Up to a point (depending on income level, age and life course and local knowledge) we can choose the neighbourhood and the kind of dwelling in which we live. But we have much less choice over who our neighbours are. Given that there appears to be quite a range of views about neighbouring and good and bad neighbours, how is some kind of accommodation reached? At the more immediate interpersonal level, this may be a matter of ongoing trial and error and negotiation. This is aided by the fact that there is considerable fluidity and flexibility within the terms of good or bad neighbour and so some kind of leeway is not only possible but essential. In addition there may be some kind of locally based norms, perhaps reinforced by local associations or informal gatherings.

There are a variety of sociological factors that have a bearing on these understandings of neighbours. An important one relates to life course especially in relation to the presence of young children of school age or younger. Children themselves have their own distinct perspectives on neighbourhoods. Elderly or retired persons might also be perceived in a particular kind of way and the same applies to single persons or childless couples. Of equal importance are questions to do with ethnicity and social class that may constitute the neighbourhood or which may overlap with it. Our concern here is less with the processes by which neighbourhoods are constructed or by which one acquires neighbours, good or bad, but with the wider significance of neighbours within the general framework of acquaintanceship.

It is clear that the experience of neighbours may cover a considerable range in terms of a variety of dimensions. These dimensions may include visibility, frequency of contact and interaction and, more generally, neighbouring careers taking into account the length of time involved and the processes within the overall experience of being neighbours. Hence any statement about their overall significance within a framework of acquaintanceship requires considerable qualification. A kind of provisional continuum may be established from 'known strangers' to 'near intimates'. Neighbourhoods may include passing or fleeting acquaintances while your neighbours may include near intimates.

Neighbours and neighbouring

Probably the most conventional understanding of 'neighbours' refers to 'next-door' neighbours. The visual image is of a row of suburban dwellings, detached, semi-detached or terraced. At various times in my life, I have lived in this kind of location. For example, I spent several years in Manchester in a large semi in a row, running from one street corner to the next, of about eight similar dwellings. On one side was a corner house, detached. On the other side (the other part of my semi) there had been three different sets of neighbours during my residence there. My small back garden backed onto the garden of someone who was known to me through our shared membership of the Labour Party. I could provide mini, if partial, biographies of most of the residents in this row. During my time in this house, there were some minor and short-lived disagreements, a certain amount of reciprocity and looking out for each other and some knowledge of others that might not always have been welcome. What knowledge I obtained of my neighbours was partly through direct observation, some sharing and visiting, some over-hearing and some through third parties. With one exception, this knowledge was confined to my side of the road. The road was quite busy and served as an effective barrier for most of the time.

Clearly, not all neighbourly relations are like this although the majority of studies seem to reflect variations on this theme. I shall, for the most part, follow the general drift of the published studies while recognizing that other living arrangements (dwellers in modern apartment blocks for example) might produce other stories and practices (see, for example, Hanley, 2008).

I have argued that while there might be some element of choice in terms of neighbourhood, there is rarely the same degree of choice in terms of neighbours. The fact that your neighbours might appear to be broadly compatible in terms of considerations to do with social class, ethnicity, age and life course and so on does not mean that they will be good neighbours. The popularity of television programmes dealing with 'neighbours from hell' bears witness to this anxiety. While students or young people in shared accommodation might vet prospective housemates, this is rarely possible in terms of other residential arrangements.

This also means that becoming a neighbour is a process that begins at the time of initial arrival and can continue for some period afterwards. This is well expressed in a study of Norwegian neighbouring. 'Somehow or other the newcomer must find out the whys and the wherefores of neighbourly togetherness. It is a process of trial and error' (Haugen and Holtedahl 1982: 4)

This process of trial and error refers to a teasing out of the informal norms and expectations of those who live next door or close by. These may be more general norms as to what is expected in this particular neighbourhood but more important are the particular expectations and interests of the individual neighbours themselves. This process is described in some detail in Gans's study of Levittown, a newly built neighbourhood where, to a large extent, everyone was a newcomer. Here there is a double process of both understanding one's immediate neighbours and developing some 'block norms' more generally (Gans 1967: 48). In the case of the former, there is a process of exchanging pieces of information about yourself and other members of your household and looking for common interests. Equally important, as Gans points out, is discovering which topics might be taboo. Gans, for example, quickly found out that his liberal views on race and religion might not be acceptable to his immediate neighbours. His neighbour, aware of the liberal views of most professors, quickly let it be known that 'he shared Southern race attitudes and was a fundamentalist Baptist' (p. 47). The sub-text was that good neighbours avoided these potentially divisive issues.

This sense of trial and error is not simply a question of avoiding potentially divisive issues or seeking out common interests. It is also a question of the degree of openness or distance that is expected. Too much openness might store up problems for the future if relations were to cool off for some reason. Too much distance might result in one being thought snobbish or standoffish. This is not simply a question of the exchange of information and views but also of the kind of access expected to the other's property, the degree and kind of expected visiting and entertaining.

22 Acquaintances

In the case of Levittown, matters were perhaps slightly simpler as most of the residents were in a similar position of strangeness. There might be a fair amount of visiting and entertaining initially when your main social resources were your more immediate neighbours. Later, individuals developed and joined more community-wide groups where they found others more compatible in terms of interests and values (Gans 1967: 124). This may be different where your neighbours are already more established and have developed more individualized patterns of visiting and entertaining.

I have argued that acquaintanceship can be understood in terms of a particular kind of knowledge that one person has of another and this certainly applies in the case of neighbours. As with other forms of acquaintanceship this knowledge will almost certainly be partial and is often based on fleeting interactions. 'Generally speaking, however, neighbours were friendly and quick to say hello to each other, although more intense social contact was limited to relatives and friends' (Gans 1965: 14). 'Many West Enders had known each other for years if only as acquaintances who greeted each other on the street' (p. 15).

However, it would be wrong to minimize the importance of this kind of knowledge. As Stokoe points out, this knowledge can be quite extensive even if you do not know the other person's name (Stokoe 2006). It does not take long to know whether your neighbour has some form of regular employment outside the home, whether there is a partner or children, whether they have pets, go to church on a regular basis or spend a lot of time on the garden. All this goes well beyond the simple categorical knowledge that is exchanged between strangers and yet may be based on little more than passing exchanges and what is immediately available to one's eyes and ears.

It is also important to point out that such knowledge does not simply arise through the encounters or sightings of the two neighbours concerned. Information about other neighbours may emerge out of dyadic conversations and gossip: 'After I mentioned being a professor, he made a crack about another neighbour, a blue-collar worker, to indicate that, although he referred to himself as "a glorified truck driver" he was, nevertheless, a white collar worker like me' (Gans 1967: 46–7). Even this single sentence can highlight processes of some complexity, establishing similarities and differences and some indications of individual perceptions of class and status. It may also be the beginning of a process of the exchange of information, placing the recipient, Gans, under some obligation to provide similar information on a future occasion.

It has already been suggested that this process of acquiring and evaluating knowledge about neighbours is not straightforward and mistakes may easily be made. Further, knowledge might be obtained in ways that are unwelcome and which might serve as a warning of potential future difficulties. Stokoe (2006) writes of 'obtrusive public intimacy' or 'non-familial intimacy' to describe this kind of less-welcome knowledge. What this means is that a neighbour is provided with a degree of intimate knowledge about the other which was not asked for or expected. This is the stuff of disputes between neighbours and which may result in interventions by the police or other external agencies. These unwanted intimacies may include nude

Acquaintances in space: neighbours 23

sunbathing, loud domestic quarrels accompanied by 'bad' language and personal accusations, sounds of sexual activity or frequent visits to the toilet (Gurney 2000).

Perhaps the most frequently cited accusation that might be levelled at neighbours is to do with 'noise'. This is a complex term, situationally defined (Stokoe 2006). Noise, like dirt, is matter (in this case, sound) in the wrong place or at the wrong time. Not all of this noise may reflect uninvited intimacies such as the sounds of domestic quarrels or sexual intercourse. Loud music or television programmes at full volume are probably high on any list of neighbourhood complaints. Similarly, people may complain about their neighbour's excessive propensity to complain about what they define as 'normal' levels of noise. However, even where the knowledge obtained is not strictly intimate, it is a knowledge (of tastes in music, for example) which is thrust upon one rather than obtained through 'normal' neighbourly exchanges. Noise might, therefore, be defined as unwelcome acquaintanceship knowledge. But it is knowledge nevertheless.

I have argued that the kind of knowledge that characterizes acquaintanceship applies in no small measure to relations between neighbours. It is partial, accumulated directly and indirectly over time and not always obtained through direct exchanges. But, however partial, it is always more than categorical knowledge. However, acquaintanceship involves practices as well as knowledge although the process of accumulating knowledge may be seen as a form of practice. Some accounts of communities describe regular visits and exchanges between neighbours over long periods of time. In 'Springdale', the community studied in *Small Town in Mass Society* (Vidich and Bensman 1958: 34) we are told that the terms 'friends' and 'neighbours' can almost be seen as standing as synonyms for 'folk'. They describe patterns of reciprocated borrowing and mutual support within a framework shaped by a public ideology of equality. Their account has strong echoes in some of the well-known studies of British rural and working-class communities.

However, it is possible that this picture has dominated popular understandings of community and, as a consequence, it is likely that many modern living arrangements might be seen as falling short of this model. Certainly some other, more recent, accounts of neighbouring suggest something slightly different: 'Unlike relationships within kin groups, links between "nigh-dwellers" are not characterized by strong norms of care or altruism. Instead, neighbourliness is based largely on reciprocity' (Perren et al. 2004: 967)

While there are clearly overlaps between this account and other descriptions of communities, there is a slight difference of emphasis. The reciprocities in many cases might be quite small and elaborated over time. In some cases, more extensive practices of informal care might be involved but it is important not to see this as being at the core of neighbourly relationships. Indeed, the reciprocities might be negative, a question of not playing loud music or of providing advance warning if some disruption to everyday routines is anticipated.

Perhaps the minimal form of reciprocity between neighbours involves mutual greetings. 'Sometimes, even relationships with directly adjacent neighbours could be restricted to an exchange of hellos' (Gans 1967: 156). These might include brief enquiries about the other's health or statements about the weather. Such greetings might be seen as ritualistic and superficial or even as lacking in sincerity. However, such fleeting exchanges imply some mutual recognition of each other as identifiable individuals, as legitimately occupying similar or linked social spaces. This is memorably described by Jane Jacobs: 'Customs vary; in some neighbourhoods people compare notes on their dogs; in others they compare notes on their landlords. Most of it is ostensibly utterly trivial, but the sum is not trivial at all' (quoted in Seabright 2005: 114).

The location of such small reciprocities is important. For the most part, they take place outside, in the street, over garden fences or in some shared semi-public space: 'The lawn is not private ground; it is an easily accessible public area. It is not the place for intimate confidences and deep commitment in the personal lives of others' (Haugen and Holtedahl 1982: 14). This comes from an account of a Norwegian suburb and clearly defines the kinds of spaces where informal exchanges can take place outside the home. Similar sites may be children's play areas close to apartment blocks or nearby shops or bus stops. What is important is that these exchanges do not take place within the home and that they occur when one or both of the parties concerned are engaged in some routine or individual project. They are not planned; they just happen. These small, public or semi-public, exchanges do not simply define ideas of neighbours or neighbourliness: they also play their part in constructing a neighbourhood.

I have indicated that neighbourliness involves some minimal and partial knowledge and some equally minimal practices. The knowledge and practices may go further but without this minimum there is no acquaintanceship. Nevertheless, even within this quite limited framework there can be some considerable variation. While some of this variation will reflect individual preferences and competences, it is also possible to sketch some more general features that shape this knowledge and practice.

Clearly, the actual design and history of the neighbourhood or collection of dwellings will play a major part. Levittown, for example, was deliberately constructed by designers who had some sense of the kind of neighbourhood that they were creating: 'Propinquity is a factor while people get to know each other, after which compatibility becomes the major criterion, but the spaces between houses and the gentle curvature of the streets put enough distance between people to allow them to ignore all but next-door neighbours' (Gans 1967: 281). Other neighbourhoods have grown up in a more haphazard fashion and the variations can be quite subtle. Some neighbours can be seen but rarely heard; others may be heard but rarely seen. It is probably not necessary to explore these complexities further but merely to indicate that they are part of the source of variations in neighbouring knowledge and practices.

Neighbourhoods are not simply shaped by their history and the design of the dwellings but also by demographics and the actual compositions of the households that are the constituent parts. Some neighbourhoods, by accident or design, may consist of people of a similar age or of similar stages in their life course. Again, we are probably not talking about determined relationships here although there is some evidence to suggest that neighbours may have greater significance for people living on their own (Washoff et al. 2005). The importance of neighbourly relationships for the elderly have been documented in several studies. Thus one study showed that people over 70 knew twice as many of their neighbours as people under 30 and 40 per cent of people aged over 70 spoke to their neighbours daily compared with a fifth for those under 30 (Mulgan and Burdett 2005).

The presence of children may have a mixed effect. On the one hand they may provide the occasion for exchanges between neighbours as topics for conversation, information and advice but, equally, they may provide sources of tension and dispute. The behaviour and appearance of children may be ways in which neighbours assess each other's social and moral status. Further, a more child-centred sociology will recognize that children themselves have their own understandings of neighbourhood and neighbours and engage in their own neighbouring practices. Children may get to know adults other than their parents or other family members through either their parents' friends or neighbours or through the parents of their own friends (Sue Milne, personal communication).

Design of neighbourhoods and the composition of the different households, therefore, play a complex part in shaping neighbourly knowledge and practices. Further complexities arise when we consider social characteristics (in addition to age and marital status) of the neighbours themselves. It is often assumed that gender is an important factor shaping neighbourliness: 'The regulation of togetherness is left to the women and it is a "task" that has to be done' (Haugen and Holtedahl 1982: 4). Indeed, one conventional image of neighbouring is of two women talking over the garden fence in the process of hanging out the washing. However, it is likely that such an image belongs more to the past, perhaps even to folklore, than to the present reality. A study of neighbouring among the elderly argues that it is not the case that men do not engage in neighbouring practices (Perren et al. 2004). Our tentative conclusion here is that gender is a factor in the elaboration of neighbour knowledge and practices but it cannot be detached from other factors to do with age and generation.

We would also include social class among the list of factors that shape neighbourliness. Crow et al. contrast the relatively loose patterns of 'contemporary neighbourliness' with the 'compulsory solidarity' of the past (Crow et al. 2002). This is in part a historical comparison with an implied reference to the classic British community studies but also reflects class differences. The suggestion here and elsewhere is that shared deprivations in terms of work (or lack of work) and income create a kind of defensive solidarity in which you come to rely on kin, friends and neighbours for support and services beyond the simple exchange of greetings. While it is far from being the case that social inequalities and poverty have disappeared it is also the case that the nexus linking work, residence and class solidarity has become considerably weakened. Evidence of locally based solidarities can still be discovered but they are not the whole story. Indeed, one study is reported as arguing that the more wealthy have a greater sense of neighbourliness than their poorer counterparts. The chief executive of the Family and Parenting Institute is quoted as saying:

For most parents, the picture is actually quite positive. There is a sense of neighbourliness, security and happiness which is far removed from the picture which is sometimes presented. But for the poorest families life isn't so rosy. They are afraid to go out at night, their children lack safe green spaces to play in and, worst of all, they feel less able to rely on the kindness of neighbours.

(Ward 2007: 9)

There are, therefore, all sorts of ways in which neighbouring practices vary and it is possible to identify some of the factors that might influence, often in quite complex ways, these practices. But a theme which emerges with some consistency in British and American studies at least, is the idea of some kind of balance between distance and closeness. We have seen, in the accounts of the process of becoming a neighbour, that learning this balance requires considerable social skills and is often easy to get wrong. Later in this chapter I shall discuss what might be called 'the ethics of neighbouring'; here I shall outline the main ideas.

Zweig, in his account of British working-class life summarized these values with the phrase 'friendly but not too close' (Zweig 1961: 116). Although this was written in 1961, very similar phrases or summaries might be discovered today. 'Friendly but not a friend' is an even more revealing idea. Quite recently, Savage et al. (2005) wrote of 'respectful distance'. In a quite different context, and possibly for slightly different reasons, Hannertz, in his account of ghetto life talked about the importance of minding one's own business. Humour and joking relationships might help to achieve this sense of distance in what might otherwise be a close context. (Hannerz 1969: 65–6). These examples can be multiplied.

A phrase which frequently occurs in British studies of neighbourhoods is: 'we are not in each others pockets'. It is worth speculating on the layers of meaning attached to pockets as a metaphor. First, pockets are areas of intimacy. They are identified with inner rather than outer space and they have a particularly intimate relationship to the owner. Items of personal or intimate significance might be concealed within pockets. At the same time, outer pockets at least also have a presence in public space. They appear in jackets, coats and trousers on the outside and are visible to others as features designed into these garments. This also means that they have a degree of vulnerability, partly because of their location and partly because of the valuable items they may contain.

So a desire not to be in each other's pockets is a desire to recognize the integrity and the distance of the other person, even – or especially – at a point of vulnerability. We recognize the appearance that the other presents to us (where they live, what they are wearing) and the way in which this represents a legitimate barrier.

Yet pockets may also symbolize resources, especially money. Potential donors to good causes are expected to dig deep into their pockets. A desire not to be in the other's pocket, therefore, may also mean that whatever practices may take place between neighbours, the lending or borrowing of money is not one of them. Or, more simply, there are limits to the kinds of claims that we may make of our neighbours and they of us.

Neighbourhoods

I have already suggested that there are differences and complex relationships between neighbours, neighbouring and neighbourhood. While one's neighbours are located within a neighbourhood, the idea of neighbourhood is more than the sum total of neighbours. For one thing, a neighbourhood is not simply composed of people but is also constructed by dwellings and other buildings, public and semi-public spaces and routes, identifiable landmarks and notices and signs. Further the people who may be found within a neighbourhood during a specified period of time might not simply be neighbours in the sense we have used up to now. Immediate neighbours and their practices can contribute to a sense of neighbourhood but neighbourhoods are locations where other kinds of acquaintances can be discovered.

Perhaps one of the most memorable accounts, providing a sense of what I understand by neighbourhood in this connection, is to be found in Jane Jacobs *The Death and Life of Great American Cities* (1969[1961]). Based partly upon her own experiences and partly upon her exploration of what makes neighbourhoods work or fail to work, this book is a rich source for the study of acquaintanceship. While recognizing that urban locations are full (for any one individual) of strangers, these strangers can become acquaintances: 'When you see the same stranger three our four times on Hudson St, you begin to nod. This is almost getting to be an acquaintance, a public acquaintance, of course' (1969: 54).

Her focus is particularly on institutions like neighbourhood shops and, especially, the sidewalks. Potentially, she argues, sidewalks of the right width and length and the people who occupy or move along them, can perform important functions. They may be a source of safety and social control, they may provide all kinds of valuable, practical contacts and they may help in the assimilation of children into a context wider than the immediate family. The point is that the others, encountered in the neighbourhood or on the sidewalk, are not intimates: 'Cities are full of people with whom, from your viewpoint, or mine, or any other individual's, a certain degree of contact is useful or enjoyable; but you do not want them in your hair. And they do not want you in theirs either' (1969: 56).

One feature of neighbourhoods is the way and the extent to which there are identifiable sub-divisions within them. This suggests that the idea of neighbourhood can be a very flexible one and may be relatively narrowly defined, consisting of 'people like us' or understood more broadly, consisting of numerous different groups of persons, perhaps constituting sub-communities. Thus Gans, describes the following types of 'West Enders' (Gans 1965: 28): the maladjusted, the middle-class mobile, the routine seekers and the action seekers. Hannertz outlines the following categories in 'Soulside': mainstreamers, swingers, street-families and streetcorner men' (Hannertz 1969: 37). One assumes that such categories, although constructed by the researchers are in some measure based upon locally available or understandable typifications. They are not referring to identifiable sub-neighbourhoods so much as to different types of people who live within a wider locality. From the point of view of my present concerns these distinctions can be important in that they can become the basis according to which differential significances of acquaintances might be identified. Thus, Hannertz's swingers, for example, might have a lifestyle where acquaintances within loose-knit social networks might be of particular importance (1969: 44). Again these acquaintances are less likely to be neighbours but may be part of the way in which neighbourhoods are constructed.

Studies of British working-class communities frequently located and often repeated a two-fold distinction between 'the rough' and 'the respectable'. In part, these can be linked to different neighbouring practices and familiar stated values such as 'friendly but not too close'. 'The rough' may serve as negative models to 'the respectable' (and vice versa) of how not to conduct good neighbourly relations so that there can be a close, mutually-reinforcing, relationship between values of neighbourliness and these divisions. 'Roughness' and 'respectability' do of course have other indicators such as the state of the gardens or front-yards, general levels of maintenance and physical appearance and levels of noise or rowdy conduct. Thus neighbourly practices can contribute to any overall sense of a neighbourhood in qualitative terms.

This distinction, and others like it, can also highlight one feature of acquaintanceship. Not only are acquaintances to be differentiated from 'friends' but relationships with acquaintances need not even be 'friendly'. A respectable resident may know a lot about her 'rough' neighbours, possibly far more than she would wish to know, and to this extent would define the neighbours concerned as acquaintances. But this knowledge does not mean that the relationship would ever be defined as a friendly one.

In some cases these folk distinctions can apply to identifiable households and there may be a certain amount of agreement, certainly among the 'respectable' as to who is who. But sometimes these distinctions may be more free-floating. In the stigmatized area of Glasgow labelled 'wine alley', individuals when confronted with this negative label would deny ownership and attribute it to people in another street or on the other side or end of a street (Damer 1989). The way in which a neighbourhood is perceived by those outside, perhaps at some distance from, that neighbourhood can impact upon the values and perceptions of the residents themselves. Neighbouring practices, real or imagined, can contribute to a sense of neighbourhood.

Hannertz defines the Ghetto way of life in these terms: 'a web of intertwined but different individual and group life styles' (Hannertz 1969: 12). This can be applied to ideas of neighbourhood more generally. These various individual and group lifestyles may contribute to a sense of class and class identity either through defining the neighbourhood as a whole in these terms or through locating positions within this neighbourhood. A sense of class position, in terms of a set of lived experiences and understandings of the world as opposed to an externally imposed category, emerges in part from where and how one works but also from where one lives. Neighbouring practices may contribute to a sense of class identity in the dual sense of coming to an understanding of others who are like oneself and of constructing a sense of who one is as an individual.

It should be stressed that even in apparently homogeneous neighbourhoods, issues of class and status, as our reference to the rough/respectable division indicated, are not simply to do with the character of the neighbourhood as a whole. Class frequently cuts across neighbourhoods as it cuts across working environments. Indeed, it is sometimes possible to argue that class identity emerges from a sense of difference from one's neighbours as much as from a sense of identity with them: 'In a middle class community then, people of working class culture stay close to home and make the house a haven against a hostile outside world' (Gans 1967: 27). In this recently constructed community of Levittown, the working-class minority may look upon the social life and community activity of the middle-class majority and conclude that this is not for them. In other words, it is likely that differing neighbourly practices may contribute to a sense of class difference.

As has already been argued, neighbourhoods are more than the sum of neighbour relations that take place within them. This includes numerous sites and locations which constitute common or overlapping points of reference. These are places which anchor the neighbourhood and provide common points of reference even if they are not actually patronized. For those who do patronize these particular institutions, they are places where acquaintances are to be found. In the part of Manchester where I lived for several years, I could cite three pubs, various shops, a Chinese takeaway, a barber's shop, a centre where adult education classes took place, a recreation ground, and so on. But there were also more subtle features such as the nearest post box or bus stops. These are places where acquaintances might develop, if fleetingly, where people may stop for a few minutes and find themselves in conversation. It is also the case that the points of contact, of common reference, also provide the material for the construction of class and other identities.

There are some affinities here between my discussion of neighbourhoods and the longstanding discussion of the nature of community. Clearly there are overlaps here. Crow and Allan define community in these terms: 'the ways in which individuals are embedded into sets of personal relationships which are based outside the household' (Crow and Allan 1994: 177). This certainly would seem to include a lot of what has been discussed in this chapter, including neighbouring practices and the development of a sense of neighbourhood. We are no longer – if we ever were – confined to an idea of a community as a strongly bounded location such as a village or a small mining town. It is the meaning of the term 'embedded' which perhaps requires further investigation. This may include being part of a network of small reciprocities and exchanges, perhaps sometimes including wider or deeper obligations. But it also includes what I see as being part of a sense of neighbourhood, the shared spaces or references points which, even where they may not be used (a pub or a church, for example) still remain as physical reminders of where one lives.

I have recently argued that one way of understanding community is in terms of a 'nexus of stories' (Morgan 2005; 2008). It is through overlapping stories that we build up a sense of where we are and where we belong. When I wrote this, I was thinking of actual stories, verbal accounts exchanged between acquaintances or intimates and about other acquaintances or intimates. I would now wish to add the ways in which these common reference points may not only be the sites where these exchanges take place but which may form part of the conversations through which neighbourhoods are reproduced. I should also wish to add the stories which one may tell oneself, the inner narratives though which one attempts to make sense of where one lives and one's location within it. This may be especially important for people who are alone, are newcomers or transients within a particular location but applies to everybody to some degree or another (Archer 2003). Embeddedness occurs through such stories and such stories are partly exchanged with acquaintances and deal with acquaintances and their locations in neighbourhoods.

Neighbourhoods are, then, not simply the sum of all the neighbours who compose them. Yet, these neighbours and the practices of neighbouring are part of the process of developing a sense of neighbourhood through the small reciprocities and daily exchanges that take place between them. Reciprocally, the neighbourhood provides the points of reference and commonalities which can be woven into conversational exchanges between neighbours.

Institutionalized 'neighbours'

Most of what I have said up to now has referred to what might be conventionally understood as neighbourhoods: rows or streets of houses, detached, semi-detached or terraced. I have said less about apartment blocks, although these are an important part of people's living experiences and probably raise slightly different considerations. A recent discussion of British housing estates shows considerable variety. There can be relative anonymity and distance, but there may also be considerable solidarity when neighbours organize in the face of an external threat (Hanley 2008).

Somewhere on the margins of the idea of neighbours and neighbourhoods are shared residences, especially those shared by students or other young people during a certain, limited, period in their life courses. There is probably a difference between the term-time student accommodation (Kenyon 1999) from which residents frequently return 'home' (i.e. to the parental home) and peer-shared households, which have a more exclusive and slightly more long-term character (Heath 2004). It is likely that, at least in Britain and similar countries, that many young people will expect to spend some of their time in peer-shared households as part of their housing careers.

Where possible, the others are people who are chosen as co-residents. Friends, or at least people with whom one has some prior acquaintance, are preferred to strangers although the practices of landlords or landladies may work against this. In some cases, existing residents may interview or otherwise vet potential newcomers. Common interests or dispositions (vegetarianism, non-smokers) might be a basis for selection. Individuals will have their own bedrooms but there will be some shared space and, frequently, some shared activities or rituals.

While a high proportion of co-residents in these peer-shared households will describe themselves as friends or as 'like a family' it is also likely that this will not always apply and that some of the others will be more like acquaintances. This may reflect the fact that these arrangements are not always stable and individuals may come and go at different paces. Nevertheless, the others are more than neighbours and the balance between distance and intimacy will be shifted more in the direction of the latter rather than the former.

Also shaping co-residence, and hence patterns of acquaintanceship, are what Goffman described as 'total institutions' (Goffman 1968[1961]) which combine residence with other practices to do with work or professional interventions. In contrast to peer-shared households, there will frequently be a strong element of compulsion involved in entering a total institution (prisons, military service) and even where this element of compulsion is muted there will be little choice, once entered, as to one's co-residents.

My own experiences as a national serviceman in the Royal Air Force (1955–57) may illustrate some themes here (Morgan 1987). I lived in a variety of billets housing from between four to about twenty airmen. I would say that I had relatively few friends (probably just one or two close friends) but a large number of acquaintances, not simply from among my co-residents in the billets but also where I worked, the canteen and the NAAFI, through my involvement in church activities and a musical appreciation group. As conscripts and other servicemen were constantly moving in and out of the different stations, there was considerable fluctuation in this wide set of acquaintances.

Knowledge of these numerous acquaintances was necessarily slanted and partial although more than simply categorical. Individuals were not interchangeable. Indeed, it was my impression that people made somewhat exaggerated, one-sided presentations of self in order to preserve some sense of personal identity in an otherwise regimented environment. John was, allegedly, from an aristocratic background and went hunting at weekends; Glenn had been a teddy boy in Edinburgh; Steve was gay; Gary was frequently drunk; Barry was, on his account, a spectacular womanizer and so on. Within the wider context of the station, certain 'characters' became well known and identified. Airmen would gossip about the activities of the officers and civilians on the station.

An example of the way in which this partial, and probably trivial, knowledge was used was through the frequent deployment of the phrase 'get some in'. The phrase meant that the recipient had less experience of service life (and hence was further away from demob day) than the initiator. In order to be able to use this phrase, participants had to know their relative lengths of service (and often the difference was quite small) well enough at least to avoid contradiction. I have argued that this apparently meaningless ranking system only had meaning in a context which was formally equalitarian and where it was not done to 'pull rank' (literally or metaphorically) on another person.

Looking more generally at total institutions (mental hospitals, prisons, military establishments, etc.) it can be readily seen that they have several important differences from the kinds of residential arrangements considered in this chapter. There is a much stronger element of compulsion; conventional boundaries between home, work and leisure disappear; people are frequently moved around in batches; and there is often a clear division between the inmates and the staff.

All this means that these are environments in which acquaintances flourish. Individuals often have plenty of time on their hands to pick up, through conversations and visual and oral impressions, partial information about other inmates and, indeed, members of staff. Closer friendships – buddy relationships and sexual liaisons – do exist although they are frequently the subject of control or official disapproval. It seems likely that acquaintanceship, as I have defined the term, is the more characteristic relationship although this itself could vary in degree from some fleeting or passing knowledge to something close to friendship or group solidarity.

Goffman's account, drawing on numerous studies or descriptions of total institutions, points to one feature which has familiar echoes. There are constraints on communication between inmates (and, one assumes, even more so between inmates and staff). Goffman refers to 'inmate etiquette' (Goffman 1968: 66), a kind of rationing of the information that one imparts to or requests from another. A good example of this is the 'sad tale' told by the prisoner or the mental hospital patient to account for their presence in that institution. Such tales are part of a selective presentation of self. They are volunteered to inmates and frequently accepted without question. He writes of 'reciprocally sustained fictions' (p. 142). Of course, such presentations are vulnerable and open to discrediting by staff or other inmates and it is perhaps this vulnerability that makes these tacit agreements so poignant.

In the case of relationships between staff and inmates other considerations arise. Members of staff may fear that too intimate a knowledge of individual inmates may undermine their attempts to maintain an orderly environment with its routines and set procedures. Further, any suggestion of favouritism might also threaten this order. From the other side, inmates may develop a code limiting communication with staff to more or less ritualized exchanges.

Within the total institutions, the patterns of loose acquaintanceship may have clear functions, at least from the point of view of the inmates. Goffman writes of the 'secondary adjustments' (1968: 56) on the part of inmates, deprived of the normal supports and escape routes available in the world outside. These are semi-covert ways of working the system, of gaining small advantages from the daily routines and practices of the institution. Some of these may be more or less individual, such as putting up pictures or other items in order to humanize and colonize one's immediate space. But others, such as learning about places where it is possible to be relatively free from staff interference, require the advice from fellow inmates, more experienced in the underlife of the institution. These are the 'free places', places marginally outside the formal procedures of the institution. These contrast with 'group territories': 'He shares the first with any patient and the second with a selected few' (Goffman 1968: 216).

All these, combined with more personal territory, go towards constituting the inmate underlife of the total institution. It is likely that loose networks of acquaintances are, for example, more effective in developing systems of 'undercover communication' and the circulation of messages than more intimate or dyadic ties (Goffman 1968: 228). Similarly the informal economy, often described in prison literature, is based upon acquaintanceship and limited reciprocities.

Hence, while the life within total institutions might seem very different from everyday experiences within neighbourhoods, there are some affinities. The idea of acquaintanceship is of even greater significance in the former and there is frequently a greater importance attached to the withholding of information and maintaining distance. Literature on total institutions (especially prisons) has often focussed upon the dyadic homosexual or lesbian relationships or hierarchies of informal control; the more everyday significance of acquaintanceship may sometimes be played down.

Conclusion

It is a truism to say that we all have to live somewhere and, in this process of occupying space, there is always some kind of balance between necessity and freedom. In the case of total institutions, the balance is heavily in the direction of the former; in the case of neighbourhoods, choice may play a greater, if often limited, part. Yet, as I have argued, even where a particular residence might be chosen, particular neighbours are more likely to be ascribed and this idea of ascription is important in the analysis of acquaintanceship.

From what has been said already it can be seen that neighbours may provide a range of informal services and these have been well documented in the literature. These include running small errands, providing loans or gifts of goods and services (the almost proverbial cup of sugar), collecting children from school or childminding or keeping an eye on one's premises when the owner is absent. These are the activities that come under the head of neighbouring and may be part of the definition of a 'good' neighbour. But it is part of the argument of this chapter that such activities are not always part of the definition of a 'good neighbour' and their presence does not necessarily define a 'good' neighbourhood.

To understand this it is necessary to develop an understanding of what might be described as the 'ethics of space'. Part of this involves striking the 'right' balance between closeness and distance. Such a balance is clearly subject to cultural variation as well as being open to individual negotiation. While, in the English language, 'close' may be a positive term and 'distant' more negative the former is not necessarily an unqualified good. People can be 'too' close and this sense is bound up with processes of the construction of individual identity and a sense of self. Even among persons defined as 'intimates' some kind of distance or formality might be valued. The following might be some of the characteristics associated with being 'too close':

- Taking over practices that are thought to be more appropriate between people understood to be intimates. In a society or a context where intimacy is prized, there are a finite number of persons who may be defined as intimates or for whom the practices of intimacy are appropriate. Those who presume on the practices of intimacy (sharing confidences, touching, offering 'excessive' help, etc.) may be seen as a threat to the carefully constructed (often over long periods of time) boundaries

between intimates and non-intimates. Such considerations come even more to the fore in the uncertain contexts of total institutions.
- Offending an individual's sense of personal space and ownership. Even some intimates (parents in relation to children, for example) may be seen as crossing these boundaries. Indeed, they may do it routinely.
- Contravening local understandings of 'proper' neighbouring. This might be shaped by considerations of social class or ethnicity.
- Inappropriate crossing of boundaries established in terms of significant (contextually defined) social divisions such as social class, gender, ethnicity or age.

Issues of the 'ethics of space' are also influenced by considerations of time. A newcomer has to negotiate appropriate boundaries of closeness and distance, perhaps by a process of trial and error. Neighbours and neighbourhoods can be understood as processes of becoming and development; the licence accorded to a long-term resident might not be accorded to a relative newcomer. Hence notions of 'too close' are affected by temporal considerations.

It cannot be stressed too much that notions of closeness and distance are locally and culturally defined and need to be the subject of comparative analysis. Nevertheless such notions can be woven into understandings of locally based identities, of who 'we' are. This may be done as a form of contrast; we are not like those people on the other side of the road who are too 'standoffish' or in each other's pockets all the time.

Hence part of the significance of neighbours and neighbourhoods is in association with the process of elaborating an ethic of place, an ethic that may have an applicability wider than the immediate locality. Another significant aspect can be in terms of the provision of a sense of ontological security. The sheer fact of having identifiable neighbours, irrespective of what they may do for each other, may be a source of comfort and security. It may reinforce a sense of everyday reality.

3 'Mates are not friends': acquaintanceship *and* places *of* work

Introduction

Adam Smith discussed a range of people between whom 'natural affections' might apply. He begins with parents and children but moves on to ever widening circles:

> Among well-disposed people, the necessity or conveniency of mutual accommodation, very frequently produces a friendship not unlike which takes place among those who are born to live in the same family. Colleagues in office, partners in trade, call one another brothers; and frequently feel towards one another as if they really were so.
> (Smith 1976 [1759]: 223–4)

A sense of continuity with and overlap between employment-based relationships and other intimate ties is striking. The notion of 'brotherhood' provides a link between these colleagues and partners on the one hand and family and close friends on the other. Such a blurring of boundaries between different classes of intimates was possibly characteristic of the eighteenth century (Tadmor 2001) but is not unknown closer to our own times.

That individuals brought together through shared employment or business should form sociable relationships over and above what is strictly prescribed by immediate practical concerns should come as no surprise. Homans' attempt to build up generalized statements about human behaviour, in particular his hypothesis about the relationship between the frequency of interaction and liking, was in part based upon the Hawthorne studies of working behaviour (Homans 1951; Roethlisberger and Dickson 1939). From these detailed and varied studies emerged the contrast between the formal system of working relationships – the one prescribed by management, perceived commercial requirements and technology – and the informal system of social relationships that developed between workers on a day-to-day basis. Here we have accounts of gossip, informal games and structured group relationships. Different workers have different numbers and kinds of informal relationships; some of these could be classified as friendships while others would be closer to acquaintanceships. One kind of difference noted was the extent to which the relationship continued outside work.

It would be fair to say, however, that many, perhaps most, of the relationships described by Roethlisberger and Dickson and several subsequent studies of factory behaviour were closer to acquaintances rather than to friends. There was some knowledge of the other (their names and nicknames and other personal characteristics) and some conversational exchanges but generally little more than that. Workers may be brought together through being engaged on similar tasks or located in similar parts of the factory or though work-prescribed interdependencies. Sometimes workers formed fairly stable cliques while in other cases the relationships were more fluid.

Detailed studies of working relationships in a variety of different settings became an important strand in the sociology of work and employment. Another influential tradition, already mentioned in a different context, was the study of communities, especially where that community was dominated by a particular industry or firm. Classic examples here were the Oscar Center studies of Gouldner (Gouldner 1955) and 'Ashton', the mining community studied by Dennis, Henriques and Slaughter (1956). Here, from the point of view of my present concerns, the main theme was one of continuity and overlap between the workplace and the community. The men you worked with were also the men you associated with in the pubs, bars and clubs where you shared much of your leisure time. Workmates were often friends and sometimes kin as well. Different kinds of overlaps between work and community were found in studies of rural or fishing communities or in studies of communities facing economic decline and unemployment. The impression that emerges from these more community-based studies is that there was relatively little time or space for 'just acquaintances'; people were either intimates (friends, family or kin) or strangers, insiders or outsiders.

Thus two important strands in industrial sociology or the sociology of work provide a slightly contradictory picture. On the one hand (especially where home and work overlap to a large extent) work may provide close and often enduring friendships. On the other, the workplace might be the basis for looser, more casual sets of relationships. The significance of such relationships might be assessed in terms of their contribution (negative or positive) to the functioning of the wider working organization but there was less assessment of their significance for the workers themselves unless they constituted friendships that persisted beyond the factory walls.

'Mates are not friends'

With the supposed decline, or at least change in the character of, community relationships it would seem that this somewhat looser structuring of informal ties at work has become the more dominant mode within modern society. This certainly seemed to be the conclusion of one of the most celebrated studies of British industrial life, the 'Affluent Worker' studies conducted by Goldthorpe et al. (1968). Here they introduced the memorable phrase, reported from workers at the Luton Vauxhall works where they conducted their study: 'mates are not friends'. A clear distinction is being made between those relationships

'Mates are not friends': acquaintanceship and places of work   37

that were structured by the workplace and more authentic intimate relationships. The former are prescribed, the latter are chosen. In some cases, of course, the physical or organizational conditions associated with factory work militate against the formation of close relationships at work. However, the argument is more one that the workers choose to make the distinction between mates and friends and choose to select the latter from outside the workplace.

The distinction between 'mates' and 'friends' which emerged from the 'Affluent Worker' studies was understood in the context of a more generalized argument about the privatized worker, whose orientation to work was more in terms of the money that it provided rather than any sense of social or job satisfaction. In fact this particular everyday formulation, or words like it, have emerged in other studies of working-class life; Goldthorpe et al. (1968) note that similar ideas were found in an earlier study by Zweig (1961). They argue that, in both cases, this is a moral statement rather than a simple classification: mates *should not* be friends.

Such a distinction seems to be very much in tune with understandings of modern working and social life. The rational instrumental world of work and employment-based relationships is contrasted with the more emotional relationships associated with family and friends. The one counterbalances the other. However, there are limits to the line of argument reflected in the phrase 'mates are not friends'. In the first place, it does not appear to be universally true. (Here, I exclude consideration of the use of the term 'mates' in Australian culture where quite different considerations come to the fore.) Indeed, there is considerable evidence to suggest that intimate relationships do frequently originate in the workplace. Figures vary: 'A survey conducted for Lloyds TSB suggests more than 70% of workers have had a relationship with someone they've worked with' (Wylie 2006). Fox notes that up to 40 per cent 'of us' met our spouses or sexual partners at work (Fox 2004: 331). More detailed, if slightly dated, comparative work was provided by Haavio-Mannila (1998) who found that 43 per cent of a sample of workers in four Northern European countries had fallen in love with co-workers at some time in the past. The point does not need labouring. Sexual relationships and intimate friendships can begin at work and these may be the basis of subsequent intimate ties.

Most of these studies, implicitly at least, focus on heterosexual relationships. There is little specifically on the kinds of male friendships that are implied by the phrase 'mates are not friends'. However, they do remind us that the borderline between work-based acquaintances and intimate relationships may be frequently crossed despite sociological models and popular moralizing that might suggest otherwise. More recent sociological analysis dealing with the sociology of emotions (especially in relation to organizations) in fact presents a more nuanced and complex account of relationships in the working environment (Fineman 2003). Further (and this will be dealt with later in this chapter) it may be that the phrase 'mates are not friends' represents a particularly masculine view of the world and does not necessarily reflect the experience of working women.

However, my main anxiety about Goldthorpe et al.'s use of the popular idea that 'mates are not friends' is not so much that it does not appear to be universally true. I am more concerned with the fact that this idea diverts attention away from our seeing work-based acquaintances as being of importance in their own right rather than simply as something that may, under certain circumstances, develop into something else. The authors of the 'Affluent Worker' studies were somewhat dismissive of the ties of work, describing them as 'a fairly superficial shop-floor *camaraderie*' (Goldthorpe et al. 1968: 60, original emphasis). In this context they seem to have relatively little significance beyond providing diversion or relieving tension. This may reflect the differences between survey based research and more detailed ethnographies.

A case study: 'Banana Time'

Rather than providing a detailed overview of work-based ethnographies I shall present a detailed re-construction of one of the classic studies of informal working groups: Donald Roy's 'Banana Time' (1960). Roy's central concern was job satisfaction and hence this research can be seen as lying within that tradition of studies concerned with exploring the human aspects of working organizations. He worked alongside a small group of workers carrying out repetitive tasks over a 12-hour working day. He had ample opportunities to observe and to join in their informal interactions, many of which will be familiar to readers of the earlier Hawthorne studies. The result is a rich, often comic, sometimes surreal or dramatic, account of interactions that might normally seem to be banal or unworthy of comment.

The work was repetitive, monotonous and exhausting, certainly to an outsider like Roy. Minimal skill was required. From the point of view of the development of and studying informal group relations, the conditions were particularly favourable, however. The group was relatively isolated and the attitudes of management seemed to be fairly 'laissez-faire'. So long as the work was done, there seemed to be little managerial interference.

I argue throughout this book that a key aspect of acquaintanceship is to do with 'knowledge' and this is clearly demonstrated in this study. In this sense, the workers were Roy's acquaintances and he was an acquaintance to them. They were also acquaintances to each other. Roy, as participant observer, was able to pick up knowledge about his co-workers, ranging from obvious information that did not require verbal interaction (bodily appearance, age, gender) to information requiring minimal interaction (names, nicknames, ethnicity) to more detailed life histories: 'Sammy, number three man in the line, and my neighbour, was heavy set, in his late fifties and Jewish: he had escaped from a country in Eastern Europe just before Hitler's legions had moved in' (Roy 1960: 159). Similar mini (albeit partial and incomplete) biographies could be reconstructed from his account of the other workers.

From the point of view of the individual worker, a major consideration was to ensure that time passed in as agreeable fashion as possible. Roy (in common with many other workers before and after him) developed little individual, mental 'games of work' to order to assist in the passing of time. But, of more interest to my present concerns are the more collective attempts to mark the passing of time.

There were a variety of short breaks and more or less ritualized punctuations of the working day. Several of these revolved around food and were given titles such as 'peach time', 'fish time' and 'banana time'. The last name can be described in Roy's own words:

> 'Banana time followed peach time by approximately an hour. Sammy again provided the refreshments, namely one banana. There was, however, no four-way sharing of Sammy's banana. Ike would gulp it down by himself after surreptitiously extracting it from Sammy's lunch box. . . . Each morning, after making the snatch, Ike would call out 'Banana time!' and proceed to down his prize while Sammy made futile protests and denunciations . . . the banana was one which Sammy brought for his own consumption at lunch time; he never did get to eat his banana.'
>
> (Roy 1960: 162)

This is perhaps the most striking of a daily sequence of rituals and the repetition of phrases and jokes. Much of this involved repetitive kidding. There were also less ritualized conversations which provided opportunities of gaining more knowledge about the others. Thus we come to learn that George's daughter had married a son of a 'professor' and this knowledge itself became part of the repetitive exchanges at work.

There are also, relatively under-explored, themes of race and gender in this account. There were some women who worked at a secluded table behind George's machine: 'Both were Negroes, and in their late twenties' (p. 160). Presumably the women were aware of the interactions between the men (including the sexual references) but were clearly not included. Race also entered into the time described by Roy as 'pick-up' time where another black man came to pick up some work and exchanged a few jokes with the men and the women. Clearly it would be possible to analyse these particular ritual exchanges in terms of the way in which they contributed to the reproduction of racialized and gendered identities. However, this is not my main concern here.

However, it is interesting to pause and explore some of the ways in which gendered identities, especially notions of masculinity, were policed on a day-to-day basis. One example was the 'poom poom' theme:

> Ike was usually the one to raise the question, 'How many times you go poom poom last night?' the person questioned usually replied with claims of being 'too old for poom poom'. If this theme did develop a goat, it was I. When it was pointed out that I was a younger man, this provided further grist for the poom poom mill.
>
> (p. 163)

In a somewhat similar vein, Sammy was sometimes ribbed for being, supposedly, hen-pecked by his wife and was frequently asked 'Are you a man or mouse?'

Themes of masculinity, woven around themes of age and marriage, were reworked and reaffirmed at some safe distance from the domestic spheres where they were presumably played out in practice.

Is this an account of acquaintanceship or of friendship? I am inclined to see it as an example of the former. For a start, there is little evidence of socializing outside the workplace. The only exception to this was Ike and George's practice of having a fish dinner together every Friday night but even this seemed to have a somewhat ritualized character. The highly ritualized and repetitive jokes and interactions might be seen as parallel to, perhaps even a parody of, the work itself, which could be seen as close to the ideal-typical alienated labour. I should also suggest that these repetitive games and phrases served to create a sense of distance which established the limits to intimacy: thus far and no further. There is knowledge of the other but this knowledge is enough to allow for the collective attempts to ensure the smooth passing of working time. Anything further in terms of intimate knowledge or other forms of intimacy might threaten this daily equilibrium. Indeed, something of the sort happened on the occasion which Roy describes as 'Black Friday'. Here some kidding (partly suggested by Roy himself) seemed to go too far and this caused the carefully sequenced rituals to break down for a short period. The ethics of work-based acquaintanceship, like the ethics of neighbouring, seem to require some kind of balance between intimacy and distance.

There might be a temptation to see these interactions as confirmation of Goldthorpe et al.'s 'superficial *camaraderie*', as lacking depth and authenticity. However, it is possible to say something more positive. Roy himself, as we have seen, links his ethnography with issues to do with job satisfaction. Katz (1968), in a re-analysis of this study, stresses the theme of (relative) autonomy which he sees as a positive force binding people together. The relative autonomy here allows the workers to bring in aspects of a wider working-class culture which assists the workers' integration into an otherwise alienating environment. I would not necessarily dissent from these interpretations but would wish to add considerations such as the development of a sense of ontological security and the shaping of a personal identity through regular exchanges with others. These are, clearly, racialized, gendered and classed identities but the analysis does not end with these categories.

The story so far

It should be clear at this point that places of employment are important sites for the development of acquaintanceship. Whether the acquaintances, or mates, formed at work are also friends is a matter for some debate. This is partly to do with local terminologies and understandings and partly a question of the ways in which particular workplaces are structured and linked to wider communities. But I should also argue that debates about whether mates are, can be, or should be, friends is beside the point. Acquaintances, whether formed at work or elsewhere, have significance in their own right. They should not be judged in terms of whether they match up to some other notion of friendship.

Groupings at work are of many kinds, ranging from relatively tightly knit groups often exercising informal controls over output and earnings to much looser networks. Some of these may be prescribed or acknowledged by management while others might be subversive of the formal, managerial structure (see Zweig 1961: 81–2). More important for the present discussion is the extent to which the working relationships are segmented, that is the extent to which they remain confined to the workplace and within working hours. Some classic community studies suggested continuities between the workplace and life outside while other studies of workplaces pointed to clear separations between work, home and leisure.

One aspect, explored in a variety of ways, is the degree of autonomy enjoyed by the employees at the workplace. Such autonomy may be formally recognized by management and built into the structuring of the working environment or it may be claimed, unofficially and without formal recognition, by the employees themselves. Whatever the basis, more autonomous working groups and sets of relationships may provide the ground for a rich elaboration of informal ties and cultures. (Ackroyd and Thompson 1999; Katz 1968). Again, 'banana time', provides a detailed account of these processes.

This autonomy, among other things, provides a framework for the elaboration of humour, joking, horseplay and repetitive use of catchphrases and nicknames (Ackroyd and Thompson 1999). Fox argues that an 'undercurrent of humour' can be found in most work situations (Fox 2004: 179) and personal experience as well as sociological studies can be produced to support this assertion. My father, for example, told me of a colleague in his department in the Post Office who came to acquire the nickname 'Rembrandt'. The reason for this was, allegedly, that he began every other sentence with the phrase 'let me put you in the picture . . .' The point about this example is that the nickname persisted long after the original event or events that gave rise to it. The use of the name could only be understood within the confines of this particular set of employees and hence was a form of local knowledge. The fact that this knowledge and usage was shared constituted one of what were doubtless numerous sets of ties, small pieces of information or misinformation, routinized practices that bound people together within this particular working environment. There is, I would suggest, a close relationship between these forms of humour and joking and the development of acquaintances at work.

It should be noted that some of this humour could seem, and perhaps was experienced as, cruel and oppressive. Being able to 'take' such humour, being the willing butt of repeated jokes and insults, might be the price of acceptance within a working environment. Such joking and kidding may have some strong gender connotations and these will be explored in the next section.

Gender, work and acquaintanceship

Part of the feminist critique of much social enquiry was that it was based upon the experiences of men although these were frequently generalized to include the whole of humanity. This seemed to be especially the case in the sociology of work and employment where women, where they were found in the workplace, were either ignored or treated as constituting a particular problem, usually associated with their positions as wives and mothers outside the workplace. Hence it might be argued that much of my discussion of the formation of acquaintances at work was based upon accounts of male-dominated working environments. We have seen, for example, how women were on the margins of Roy's (1960) study. What kind of picture might have emerged had there been a woman sociologist working in the same department?

There are two issues that emerge when taking a more gendered perspective on relationships at work. The first is to do with gender as difference; are there significant differences between the ways in which men relate to each other at work as compared with working women? The second is to do with gender as hierarchy and power. Do informal relationships between men (and between women and between women and men) serve to perpetuate inequalities between men and women?

David Collinson's 1992 study contains much material that will be familiar to the readers of Roy's earlier account. Again we find accounts of humour and horseplay and the use of nicknames (Collinson 1992). However, his account is informed not only by feminist-inspired studies of the workplace but also by subsequent discussions about men and masculinities in relation to work and employment. Hence, he argues that these informal practices have many dimensions and meanings other than simply helping to make the working day pass more easily or of making oppressive relationships slightly more palatable. These practices may also be forms of resistance to managerial control although within a limited framework. They may be a form of control over other workers, a means of achieving conformity to certain standards of masculinity. New workers (and researchers) are tested to see if they can 'take' the kidding and the practical jokes. The apparent freedom may conceal a double conformity to managerial controls and to hegemonic masculinities.

We know relatively little about his workers' lives outside the workplace. This may have been a deliberate choice on his part as a researcher or it may reflect a general acceptance of the 'mates are not friends' model. We are told that: '. . . Dave build an impenetrable psychological wall between "public" and "private" life' (Collinson 1992: 95). However, it is difficult to work out from his account whether this applies more generally. Where there did seem to be some flow between the spheres of home and work it was around a more general assent to the ideas of being the main breadwinner or provider.

Collinson's study was written within a context in which much of the debate and analysis was stimulated by feminist scholarship and the wider critique of 'malestream' sociology. In the 1980s there was a cluster of British workshop ethnographies, written by women and exploring the conditions and experiences of women in the workplace (Cavendish 1982; Pollert 1981; Porter 1983; Westwood 1985). A core concern of these studies dealt with the interplay between class and gender (or, more globally, between capitalism and patriarchy) on the shop floor and the immediate environment. However, these studies also provided fascinating insights into everyday life within a factory environment and seemed to provide a useful corrective to the studies of men which had dominated the sociology of work previously. Here, I shall concentrate on two of these studies (Cavendish 1982; Westwood 1984) and attempt to explore what they can contribute to the study of acquaintanceship.

The first point is that these studies seemed to deny the generality of the argument that 'mates are not friends'. This particular formulation was not recorded by these researchers even if the term 'mates' was often used to describe these associations at work. Westwood (1984) claims that 'friend' was the most common term to be used, followed by 'sisters' or 'mates'. These friendships were not simply dyadic, brought about by spatial proximity, but contributed to a general workshop culture. This theme was particularly marked in Westwood's study of a hosiery factory in Leicester where we find jokes and singing, sharing food, celebrations and ceremonies and something of an informal economy (p. 90). Relatively light managerial controls may have contributed to the elaboration of this culture which did not appear to the same extent in the earlier, and rather different, study by Cavendish (1982). Some twenty years prior to these studies, I noticed similar patterns of sociable relationships among women working in a northern electrical components factory (Morgan 1969).

One important feature about these relationships was that they did not stop at the factory gates. Cavendish gained considerable insights into the lives of her fellow workers in terms that transcended the work/home divide. She gained insights into the way in which they dressed, their family lives, their values and religion and their life histories. She noted that several of her co-workers had already known others working in the factory before they themselves came to work there.

Westwood, like Cavendish, was invited to participate in the lives of the workers outside the factory. She has, for example, a detailed account of a hen party (including a lot of drinking, ribaldry and a male stripper) in a local pub. This continued on from pre-wedding rituals carried out (again with much laughter and many sexual references) within the factory itself. The emphasis of these studies stressed the continuity of women's lives as they moved back and forth between home and work and, in time, underwent various life transitions.

These friendships and collective activities were seen to be of considerable significance to the workers themselves. Westwood uses terms like 'sisterhood' and 'support networks' for example (pp. 80–1) while recognizing other divisions in terms of race and age. However, she also suggests that there was an ambiguous relationship between these friendships and activities on the shop floor and the worker's, more private, home lives. In many cases, this shop-floor culture was in opposition to the more restricted experiences in marriage and the family, where the experiences were sometimes oppressive or violent. However, at the same time, the workshop was a place where aspects of femininity and domesticity were celebrated, especially where weddings or children were concerned. It was as if home life underwent a kind of transmutation within the working environment. And here, perhaps, there are some affinities with the studies of men at work where some aspects of masculinity are affirmed or tested.

Are we to conclude, therefore, that men tend to have acquaintances at work while women have friends? This would be too premature a conclusion. For one thing we do not know the significance of these work-based relationships within the women's general range or networks of intimates and acquaintances. To gain this knowledge would require a different kind of research project. Further, there is evidence that there were also acquaintances (even if the term might not be used) at work in addition to friends. The following two quotations from Cavendish's (1982) study illustrate this: 'From Rosemary's bench you could see everyone in the main assembly, all 200 of them' (p. 15). It seems unlikely that any single worker could describe 200 other workers as 'friends'. The following description seems more relevant:

All the women said 'good morning' to each other and acknowledged the other several times a day. The atmosphere was warm and supportive, so no one was left out. If you passed someone in the corridor or the loo whom you had seen a couple of times and just about recognised, you would say 'hello' to them.

(Cavendish 1982: 56)

Again we are not dealing with intimates here, but these exchanges (like similar exchanges in the street or neighbourhood) have their own importance. When people say that 'X' is a friendly place to work at, they are partly referring to these more fleeting exchanges as well as to the closer friendships which may also be established.

It is possible that the idea of acquaintanceship becomes more important across the gender divide which frequently maps on to other workshop based hierarchies. Thus Westwood refers to a manager, John, using 'joking relations as a way of managing tension in the shop-floor' (Westwood 1985: 27). This is clearly something different from the jokes shared by the workers themselves; 'joking relations' reproduce differences and inequalities as well as being based upon a kind of pseudo-mutuality. John was popular but almost certainly not likely to be considered as a friend by any of the workers. Similar observations may be used in relation to the use of flirtation between those in charge and the workers at the bench. Of course, there are dangers here, and flirtation or sexualized banter across gendered hierarchies can easily slip into sexual harassment. Here a foreman or a management may be an acquaintance but an unwelcome one.

Cavendish (1982) also points to acquaintances across gender lines, referring here to the labourers and maintenance men who were also employed in her department. For the most part the relationships between the women workers and the men was friendly although, again, it seems unlikely that these constituted close friendships. In the case of those in authority, Cavendish as participant observer had some partial knowledge of charge-hands although the relationship could not be regarded as a friendly one (p. 80). When she describes, to herself, a couple of managers as 'Tweedledum' and 'Tweedledee' (p. 96) this can be seen as a form of acquaintanceship in as much as they are distinguished from other men who might pass through the workplace. My argument is that such relationships form part of the working context which contains acquaintances as well as friends.

The various workshop ethnographies that I have considered, whether they deal with men or with women, cannot be said to be a representative sample; each was conducted by particular researchers, with particular research problems, and in distinct historical periods. It would be difficult to move from these studies to generalizations about men, women and acquaintances. For example another, more recent study of a different kind of working environment suggests a different picture. Lewis (2005) talks about 'communities of coping' among nurses working in a special baby care unit. She elaborates ideas of 'collective' or 'philanthropic' emotional labour within this kind of working environment, one where we are dealing with highly charged questions of infant's lives and well-being. However, she also points out that while friendships did develop, there was also an ethos of distance, perhaps because the context was so emotionally charged. Routine exchanges might be limited to questions such as 'are you all right?' This does not contradict the picture to emerge from studies of more routine manual work but does suggest that different kinds of working environments could produce different outcomes in terms of the balance between friendship and acquaintanceship. To return to the more general theme of the section, gender is clearly a major theme in the analysis of workshop acquaintances although the complexities have yet to be explored. Numerous other studies have shown how working environments reproduce and modify gender differences and inequalities and the patterns of informal relationships, friends and acquaintances are part of these processes.

Other social divisions

What can be said about gender can also be said about other social divisions in terms of, say, class, age and ethnicity. Indeed, some of these themes are treated, interacting with gender, in the studies by Cavendish, Westwood and others. Race and age/generation certainly influenced the patterns of friendships developed at work and the extent to which there was continuity in the relationships between home, work and leisure. Possibly, therefore, relationships across ethnic or age/generation lines were more likely to be closer to the idea of acquaintanceship being elaborated in this book. But this does not mean that these relationships are without significance.

In the case of class and status we are frequently dealing with divisions based upon the way work is organized: divisions between management and workers, professionals and administrators, white collar and blue collar. Class and status, therefore, are not divisions which are possessed by employees and brought to the workplace but are divisions that are generated and reproduced within the workplace although they may well have resonances in the wider community. Such structural divisions within the workplace may impinge upon the discussion of acquaintanceship in a variety of ways:

- Relationships across these class and status lines tend to come closer to ideas of acquaintanceship rather than to friendship. As we have seen in the studies by Westwood and Cavendish (among others) a manager or a foreman may be friendly but not a friend. This acquaintanceship may range from the most fleeting fragments of information or passing recognitions to something more detailed. Thus manual workers may know the names or nicknames of their supervisors and some of the more junior managers and may, collectively or individually, elaborate little pen-portraits of them. Gossip about supervisors, managers and so on may form part of the everyday flow of conversation between workers on the shop floor.
- It is likely that there will be a lack of reciprocity. Supervisors and managers may not always know the names of the shop-floor workers (especially if labour turnover is high) while workers are more likely to know the names of managers and supervisors. Further, there are inhibitions

(heightened when issues of sexual harassment come on to the agenda) against getting too friendly or being seen to have favourites.
- Patterns of informal socializing, on and off the workplace, will also take place within supervisory or managerial groups. Some of these relationships may be characterized as friendships, others as acquaintanceships. Although these relationships have been less studied than those on the shop floor it is likely that they are of equal variety and significance (see Dalton 1959). In some cases there may be a degree of instrumentality, in terms of potential promotions and upward mobility. In some cases, as in the relationship between an older and a more junior manager, they may take on a quasi-familial character (Roper 1994).
- Within particular status groupings, gossip may play an especially important role. The 'gossip triangle' (A gossips to B about C) is part of the elaboration of complex networks of acquaintances and friends (Bergmann 1993) within the workplace. To participate in gossip is to be recognized as an acquaintance and the object of this gossip is also part of the process of the development of knowledge and acquaintanceship. Gossip is one of the practices of acquaintanceship and may be of particular importance in hierarchically structured organizations (see also Gluckman 1963).

Doubtless there is a lot more that could be said about work, acquaintanceship and these various social divisions. These social divisions, with their differences and inequalities, may stimulate the elaboration of acquaintanceship just as the practice of acquaintanceship may contribute to the reproduction (or modification) of these divisions. What may be of particular interest is the development of acquaintanceship across these various dividing lines. These weak ties (often little more than fragments of information or misinformation) are probably more likely across these divisions than friendships. Nevertheless, they have their own interest.

Changes in work and the development of acquaintances

The use of old (some of them over 50 years old) studies of working practices in the investigation of acquaintances at work has some value in laying out some of the terms of this part of the investigation. However, changes in the organization of work over the period since, say, Donald Roy's study and the present day may well have an impact on the nature and significance of acquaintanceship. Good general assessments of these changes and the debates surrounding them are readily available (see Bradley 2000). Here I shall focus on a few of these changes with the aim of assessing their significance for my discussion of acquaintanceship at work.

Fluidity and flexibility

These are key words in the discussion of late modern working practices. As with many such words, the meanings themselves may be elastic but the contrast is with notions of a relatively stable, hierarchically structured working environment, the idea of a job for life or a lifelong career and, often, clear divisions between home and work. In practice, and taking a somewhat longer historical view than simply the period from the end of the Second World War to the present day, these constructions of the past may themselves be criticized.

Flexibility is revealed in a variety of ways. In the course of a working life, an employee (at whatever level of the hierarchy) might expect to work in different positions or places or for different employers. While employed at a particular place, an employee might be moved between sites and tasks. Practices such as hot-desking and some measure of home-working might increase this sense of flexibility, in the sense of a weaker association between paid employment and notions of time and space. Some of these supposed trends might be exaggerated (the idea of a working portfolio rather than a career, for example) although the important fact is that they are increasingly understood to be part of the wider labour and employment scene.

What might be developing as a consequence of these, and other, changes is considerable flexibility in the notion of work itself. Smith et al. (2005), for example, note the considerable range of forms of social participation available to young people other than paid employment, although many of these may exist in association with some form of paid employment. These range from formal and informal voluntary work to more general notions of social participation and altruistic acts. Pettinger et al. (2005) similarly talk about the weakening boundaries between work and non-work as in forms of voluntary and community work. Elsewhere, in catering and retail for example, there may be fuzzy boundaries between work and leisure (Pettinger 2005).

Perhaps this fuzziness has been present for some while, at least in certain sectors of the economy. Consider, for example, the after-work drinks ritual, described briefly by Fox (2004: 201–2). This is work related in that those participating have a shared work environment in common and that some of the talk will also relate to issues at the workplace. Yet, they take place outside work, are not paid, and are clearly distinct from working practices. However, such practices might be part of the informal (at least) expectations of the workplace such that employees should be prepared to socialize with clients outside working hours (Rasmussen 2005).

The service economy

One long-term shift in the nature of the economy which has received much attention has been the development of the service sector. As this involves work where interaction with members of the public is central to the job description rather than incidental to it, one might assume that this involves an enlargement of the significance of acquaintanceship. In practice matters may be more complicated. For one thing, the service sector is not, sociologically speaking, an undifferentiated entity. There would seem to be a world of difference between, say, the Savile Row tailor and the worker at a supermarket checkout or in one of the major coffee-house chains.

Let us begin with two illustrations of service work, both taken from fairly recent newspaper articles. The first is a discussion of the Spanish concept of 'trato' which appeared in the *Financial Times* (Eyres 2005). The author notes that this is a difficult word to translate: 'It covers many aspects of the intercourse and dealings people have with each other . . . the way people treat each other, the way they greet, interact, pass the time of day with others, especially in commercial contexts. Trato includes, but is much broader than, the concept of service.' Much of this would seem to be to do with the development of acquaintanceship of, in this case, moving the customer out of the category of consumer and stranger. The complexities arise where service workers are trained to develop these skills in relation to their clients or customers (Hochschild 1983). But from the perspective of the study of acquaintanceship, does it matter whether the performance is authentic or not, if indeed it is possible to make this distinction?

A second example comes from an interview with a Mayfair doorman, published in the *Observer Magazine* (Rayner 2007). This gives some brief insights into the acquaintanceship work that is required by someone in this kind of position:

> I have diaries from my very first day in the job at the Ivy. I write down the colour of people's cars, what their husbands or wives look like. Sometimes I write down a name for a week just to help me remember it and when I get a quiet moment I flick through.
>
> I learnt early on that you should never get familiar with the celebrities. Building up relationships with bodyguards and chauffeurs is the way to go.

As with cab drivers, he has to learn to read signs (when someone is going to tip, for example) and to be prepared for the unexpected. He gains access to a lot of people's secrets and has to maintain a balance between friendliness and distance.

Discussions of the ways in which people 'do' service work has been at the heart of recent analyses of 'emotional' and 'aesthetic' labour. Within this framework, the apparent differences between the world of the Mayfair doorman and those of staff in coffee shops, bars and supermarkets become less important than the overlaps. While acquaintances (as opposed to friends or strangers) are built into the work itself, acquaintanceship has to be worked at. Eyres, for example, found examples of 'trato' in his local supermarket and pub (Eyres 2005). Clearly some service situations are more structured by the way in which the work is designed and managerial controls than others. People who work in pub restaurants and the bar say they prefer the greater informality and the opportunities to 'be oneself' of the latter rather than the former (Seymour and Sandiford 2005). However the work of acquaintanceship, whether spontaneous or trained, authentic or otherwise, is part of the developments within the service economy.

This is not the whole story, however. As with other working situations, the service economy involves relationships between the employees themselves as well as between employees and clients/customers. All kinds of factors – unsocial hours, the pressure of work – may contribute to the development of sociable relationships between workers in the service sector, but the clear division between worker and customer is one of these. Seymour and Sandiford's study of workers in public houses note the importance of out-of-hours socializing and the way in which these regular interactions provide social support and approval, 'social validation' (Seymour and Sandiford 2005). In part these sessions may gain some meaning in contrast to some of the unreasonable demands of customers or managers, although regular local customers may join in on occasions. In a rather different, and probably more threatening location, a job centre, Bishop et al. describe the 'communities of coping' in the case of violence on the part of clients (Bishop et al. 2005). These studies not only remind us that the customers can be unreasonable, unpleasant or even violent but that also informal social mechanisms exist to provide some degree of social support between employees. Even where customers are not violent or over-demanding, they still involve the effort of emotional and aesthetic labour on the part of the employees who develop collective and individual ways of dealing with these pressures. Given the high-turnover and the casualization of some service sectors, it seems likely that acquaintanceship, rather than friendship, is part of the relationships between employees as well as between them and their customers.

Disembodied labour

An aspect of the service economy that has been given considerable attention in recent years has been the development of disembodied labour, symbolized by call centres. Increasingly, much everyday contact with service providers is conducted over the telephone rather than through face-to-face encounters. From the point of view of the clients, such encounters would seem to be very much on the borderline between strangers and acquaintances. In some cases, the only knowledge that a client has of the person at the other end of the line is limited to accent and gender together with first name.

While popular, largely hostile, discussion of these disembodied encounters has focussed on the clients, sociological treatment has looked at the workers themselves. They have, for example, explored the emotional labour involved and the ever-present tension between quality and quantity (Brannan 2005). There has also been some attention to attempts to depart from the idea of a pre-arranged script and to make more use of informality (Bone 2006). Probably many of the considerations that apply generally to service workers or those engaged in emotional labour also apply here.

However, from our point of view an interesting line of enquiry is the way in which workers in call centres develop some ongoing knowledge of their customers which is probably enough to move them from strangers to acquaintances. In May 2007, the *Independent Extra* devoted several pages to brief interviews with people who worked on different kinds of helplines (*Independent Extra*, 2007). In some cases the knowledge developed of callers tended to constitute generalized typifications: regulars, people who just want to talk and so on. But, in these accounts, individuals appear:

- a lady whose washing machine was blocked up with £20 notes (Dyson Helpline);
- 'we have regular callers, some very nice and some not so nice' (BBC Information Line);

- an elderly gentleman who had been widowed and never used a washing machine before (Proctor & Gamble helpline).

These memorable individuals constitute talk-worthy topics for the workers and reduce the sense of distance. However, distance is important. 'Sometimes people just want to chat. We try to keep the conversation to advice though' (Procter & Gamble helpline). A worker on the UK Insolvency helpline says that he prefers to give advice on the phone where there is none of the confusing body language.

I have identified certain changes in the way in which work is organized and which might call into question the picture presented by some of the classic studies in the sociology of work. These were a growing flexibility in the way in which work is organized and fluidity in the way in which work is defined, the continuing and complex growth of the service sector (including emotional and aesthetic labour) and the development of more disembodied work situations, symbolized by the growth of call centres. Cumulatively these, and other changes, might reasonably be supposed to have an impact on the size, nature and significance of work-based acquaintances.

Overall, it can by hypothesized, these changes have led to an increase in the number of acquaintances that any one individual might have, especially when taken over the life course. Thus the fluidity and flexibility that we find in some areas of work mean that individuals move in and out of more work or quasi-work situations and that this should lead to an overall increase in the number of acquaintances over a working life course. The growth of service occupations not only means that individuals gain more acquaintances from their clients and customers in the course of their work but that 'doing acquaintanceship' (an aspect of emotional and aesthetic labour) is at the core of the employees' job description. Similar observations may be made in relation to the development of more disembodied work.

A common criticism of much of this newer kind of service work is that, with the emphasis on presentation and performance, the work has a kind of inauthenticity. Although this kind of critique has become associated with the title of Arlie Hochschild' s book, *The Managed Heart* (1983) a much earlier study by C. Wright Mills of the 'new' white-collar workers raised a somewhat similar point: 'The salesman's world has now become everybody's world, and in some part, everybody has become a salesman' (Mills 1956: 161). By now this kind of inauthentic performance is widely recognized and frequently parodied; the 'have a nice day' phenomenon.

However, a more nuanced understanding of the service sector might question the moralism of this critique. More specifically, the notion of acquaintanceship can help us to think of such encounters in the service sector more positively. If an employee (a waiter, a shop assistant) puts on a good performance this may not only be recognized as such by the customer but actually appreciated in its own terms and not as a debased form of some more intimate relation. Further, it is likely that the employee will also get caught up in the performance and will enjoy the minor sense of accomplishment.

Encounters with clients can go wrong. They can be emotionally distressing or even violent. Relationships with co-workers can provide small communities of care and social support in these cases. But, more benevolently, such encounters with clients (successful as well as unsuccessful, pleasant as well as disagreeable) may provide the basis of narratives which may be elaborated and shared with co-workers. The everyday humour and joking at work may incorporate accounts of dealings with members of the public and the judgements made can be harsh, cruel or sympathetic. There is a kind of reciprocity between the passing acquaintances developed in the course of carrying out ones daily work and the interactions with others who are similarly engaged.

Are these work-based acquaintances, mates (in the limited sense used in this chapter) or friends? Much will depend upon factors to do with the characteristics of the employees (age, stage in the life-cycle, gender, ethnicity and so on) and the workplace. Casualization, shift-work and high labour turnover may mean that such interactions, although important at the time, will remain at the level of acquaintances. More stable work settings might encourage friendships that extend beyond the workplace. Overall, however, there is a good case for arguing that changes in the organization of work favour the development of acquaintances and the elaboration of more complex forms of acquaintanceship practices.

Conclusion

From time to time in this chapter, I have alluded to possible 'functions' of these work-based relationships and practices. Certainly much of the literature seems to be full of this kind of analysis, even if the word is not always used. Thus, going to the pub after work might be functional for the organization in that it develops an attachment to the workplace as well as for the employees themselves. But it may also reproduce divisions that may be harmful to the effective working of the organization or to individuals; divisions between management and workers, men and women, different ethnic groups, and so on. This kind of analysis may be part of the analysis of the significance of acquaintanceship at work but is not the whole story.

One aspect of the more instrumental character of acquaintanceship is to do with the extent to which it may assist individuals to advance in their chosen area of work. The theory and practice of 'networking' is well understood and much analysed and this particular aspect of the use of weak ties has long been recognized in the literature. Acquaintances can be sources of information about career opportunities, about gaining recognition or simply about those little bits of information and understanding that are essential to the successful performance of a job. This kind of networking has, for example, been seen to be important in artistic circles such as the 'Bloomsbury Group' (Lang and Lang 1988; Morgan 1982). Bain, for example, shows how, as is well known, there are clusters of artistic activities in certain downtown areas. But although they cluster together, they tend to work in isolation and maintain distance. However, there is some sharing of information in the relatively brief encounters that take place between artists and this, although small, may be important in continuing in these chosen fields of work (Bain 2005).

From one point of view, the potential instrumentality of work-based acquaintances may have slightly negative connotations when compared with the more personal ties associated with friendship. I should prefer to see the matter the other way around. While acquaintances based upon work can have this instrumental character, their importance lies in the fact that they are rarely simply this, that even a one-off transaction may have some minor secondary elaborations, which distinguish such exchanges from, say, ordering goods over the Internet.

Of course, as we have seen, work-based acquaintanceships may have little or no practical significance and that they come closer to the model of 'pure sociability' (Pettinger 2005). Yet even here there may be some wider significance. For example, such contacts may provide employees with brief and partial insights into other worlds, beyond their immediate family or locality. We may remember the case of 'Sammy' in the 'banana time' study who had escaped from Eastern Europe just before Hitler's troops moved in (Roy 1960). What might otherwise seem to be rather remote 'current affairs' take on a slightly closer character through such encounters. This should not be exaggerated, but at least there is the potential for a greater empathetic understanding of the impact of world events.

Finally, and possibly most significantly, we can see the importance of acquaintances at work as part of the process of constructing everyday life. People frequently talk of the 'atmosphere' at work; 'the blokes are fine', it's a 'friendly place' and so on. I would argue that it takes more than particular friends to make for a friendly atmosphere. The number and variety of acquaintances, and the various practices that take place between them, have their significance as well.

4 Relations between professionals *and* clients

Introduction

In some ways the relationships between professionals and clients might be seen as being close to a pure type of acquaintanceship. It is clear that such relationships are not relationships between strangers, certainly not after the initial encounter. In many cases the client may have some knowledge of the professional even prior to a first meeting. At the same time, the relationships between professionals and clients are not intimate relationships although they may have some aspects of intimacy, physical, emotional and/or in terms of a particular kind of knowledge of the others' body, financial circumstances, emotional state or legal concerns.

However, this intimacy although it may have its own intensity is also subject to serious limitations. Opportunities for physical intimacy should not be used to initiate sexual relationships, the knowledge obtained about a client should not be used for other purposes and emotional insights should not be the basis for further intimacies. Such potentialities are frequently subject to professional codes and professional sanctions and in this respect the sense of a balance between intimacy and distance is built into the professional-client relationship to a degree that is rare in other acquaintance relationships.

At the same time there are clear differences between professional-client relationships and the other kinds of acquaintances that we have considered. Chief here is the clear lack of reciprocity. Whereas in other kinds of acquaintanceship, there is frequently some kind of exchange taking place and the parties may have knowledge of each other, different or overlapping, in roughly equal measures, this is not the case in professional client relationships where, frequently, the very base of the relationship is that the former is being consulted on the basis of knowledge and skills thought to be lacking on the part of the latter. This lack of reciprocity proceeds throughout the relationship over time. The professional frequently initiates interactions and leads the questions; the client is profiled in standardized records, which are built up over time. While the client may pick up some knowledge of the professional this is usually partial and fragmentary although it does have many of the characteristics of acquaintanceship. However, the client is frequently one among many, yet to the client, the particular doctor, priest or lawyer is distinct and individual. On these bases, as well as on several others, there is a clear power differential between the two.

Of course, even within medical encounters, not all doctor-patient meetings are identical. Some may be frequent, repeated and potentially fateful. Here, the knowledge built up over time, although different in kind and detail between the two parties, may be quite considerable. Other encounters might arise in the process of conducting what Strong calls 'medical errands' (1977). These errands are mostly trivial and matters to be concluded as quickly as possible. They may include getting a flu injection, collecting a prescription or having a routine dental check-up. Many of the encounters that are involved in completing medical (or other) errands are closer to the fleeting encounters discussed in Chapter 6. However, as with these other encounters, these short-lived acquaintances may have their importance as part of a sequence of short-term engagements with the outside world.

We can see that there are some overlaps here with other kinds of acquaintanceship discussed elsewhere in this book. In part, of course we are dealing with work relationships, especially from the point of view of the professional who is engaged in a particular form of people-work. The professional also, again unlike the client, is involved in a set of other work relationships, frequently unobserved by the client. Although, as Wadel has reminded us, clients themselves are engaged in a form of work it is not equivalent to the employment relationships experienced by the professional (Wadel 1979). In other words, although clients are expected to deploy all kinds of interpersonal skills in order to be able to present themselves as serious clients, the 'work' they perform is not part of a structured set of employment relations.

Again, there may be some similarities with passing acquaintances especially where there is some regularity of contact between the two parties as in the case of physiotherapy or psychoanalysis. Or there may be some similarities with fleeting encounters where the professional is only encountered once (a doctor on holiday, for example). Given that the boundaries between professionals and service occupations may be very fluid, with the latter frequently aspiring to the status of the former, the occasional or infrequent relationship with a professional may be not unlike several other encounters in urban society. Yet again, in more 'traditional' or more rural type communities the professional may also be a neighbour. In short, in dealing with professional-client relationships we are dealing with a variety of forms of and bases for acquaintanceship. Yet also, professional-client relationships have their own special features which warrant special treatment.

In this chapter I shall consider, briefly, some themes that emerge from the literature dealing with professions and professionalism, which might be especially relevant to my concerns. I shall then focus on what can, for these purposes, be seen as the core of this relationship: the consultation. Finally, I shall consider some modifications to this loose model of professional encounters.

Professional themes

Before moving to a more general discussion, perhaps some autobiographical notes might be helpful. These deal entirely with medical encounters; encounters with other professionals such as lawyers or accountants came much later in my life. The first doctor I can remember was a Dr Thompson, an avuncular Scot smelling rather agreeably of pipe tobacco. I saw him, accompanied by my mother at least initially, in his surgery in a slightly melancholy house surrounded by trees and shrubs or in the course of the home visits that accompanied the usual sequence of childhood ailments. I think that my mother thought highly of him and he seemed to have a good reputation in the London suburb where he was based. I have slightly fewer memories of Dr Hunter, another Scot, who replaced him.

The next GP I remember was in Manchester after I was married and had a full-time appointment at the university. He was in a group practice (so I was not always able to make an appointment with him) but was much preferred by me and other family members as well as other people living locally. He was humorous, sympathetic and seemed to have a good knowledge not only of my immediate family but also of other members of my department who were also patients. A copy of a sociology textbook, which several of us had written jointly, was sometimes seen on his bookshelf.

Since leaving Manchester, my medical encounters have been few and brief. I know the names of a couple of the doctors at my group practice but have only a fleeting knowledge or remembrance of them. Indeed, many of my encounters in the practice have not been with doctors at all but with nurses who give me flu injections or take my blood pressure. Even a couple or so more recent visits to a doctor with a nasty chest infection have been relatively brief.

My medical encounters have not been confined to general practitioners. I could write a similar account of encounters with dentists and some complementary practitioners including an acupuncturist. Such an autobiographical approach to medical encounters might not only trace my own embodied life course but wider historical trends. My earliest encounters were before the advent of the British National Health Service and since the establishment of this service there have been numerous changes and transformations both within and outside. The doctors that form part of my career as a patient – Doctors Thompson, Hunter, Goodman and more recent individuals – could all be seen as acquaintances within my definition of the word but they all existed within slightly different sets of relationships.

To return to more academic approaches, it can readily be seen that there is an extensive literature on professions and professionalization in existence. Moreover, in the past at least, these themes have attracted the attention of many important sociological thinkers, Parsons and Everett Hughes, for example. It is neither possible nor necessary to deal with this literature at any length but I shall merely identify some trends that have some bearing on acquaintanceship.

The first broad trend is one that has moved away from a largely functional, ideal-typical model of the professional and the nature and basis of professional practice and knowledge. Some of these accounts, in retrospect, seem too closely to mirror the professionals' own self-definitions and self-images. If the word 'professional' has become a word which is widely used to connate the responsible use of skills and knowledge, this is perhaps a measure of the success with which professionals have established their position within society over time. The emphasis in many of these attempts to construct ideal-typical models of the professional deal with such matters as specialized training and bodies of expertise, systems of internal validation and a certain degree and kind of detachment. While these themes have not disappeared from the literature, they have been partially replaced by a slightly more questioning or sceptical approach which sees many of the statements about professionals as particular kinds of claims which have their validity as claims rather than as straightforward reflections of reality.

Part of the shift has been towards an exploration of the processes of professionalization. This may be at a general historical level whereby professionals become recognized (and more numerous) collectivities within the social division of labour and, indeed, within the wider class and status system entering into, for example, systems of social classification based upon occupational titles. This is a long-term historical process which is by no means at an end. Or the concern may be more at the level of an individual occupation and the processes by which members within this occupation struggle for the official recognition that constitutes the attainment of professional status. This is part of what MacDonald and others refer to as the 'professional project' (Macdonald 1995). Macdonald clearly links his discussion to considerations of class and status through stressing the processes of social closure whereby professionals successful control entry and define what is to count as good professional practice.

We may also identify a growing interest in the perspectives and understandings of clients and with this have emerged more critical discussions of professional ethics. To some extent we may see here links with earlier sociological models where a code of practice, accompanied by the legitimatized sanctioning of those who depart from this code, was very much part of the professional self-definition. However, more recent discussions may represent this growing scepticism about the claims of professionals or those who would aspire to professional status and, in particular, the impact of interest and pressure groups based upon social divisions such as gender, race, sexuality or disability. We may also see the changing relationships between the state and the professions, especially those employed within the public sector. Indeed, in the face of particular pressure groups struggling for recognition, increasing state regulation and surveillance and the rise of consumerism informed by the media and the Internet, the early debates about and models of professions and professionalism might seem to be under serious threat.

This chapter, therefore, is being written in the context of some serious challenges to the ideas and practices associated with professionalism. However, the long and complex histories of professions and the debates and struggles associated with professional claims and counter-claims highlight something distinctive in the professional-client encounter. This very brief account of some of the themes within the analysis of professions may provide a background for a more focussed discussion of the overlaps and differences between professional-client relationships and acquaintanceship.

Professions, professionalization and acquaintanceship: the consultation

From the point of view of acquaintanceship it is argued that the consultation is at the core of the professional-client relationship. The very use of the word suggests something distinctive about this relationship. While we may consult with workmates, neighbours as well as with intimates, these encounters would rarely be described as consultations. The term conveys a sense of a set of more or less formal expectations on both sides and a sense of premeditation and planning. In addition it also implies a certain lack of reciprocity. Whether this lack of reciprocity can also be characterized as an imbalance of power is a complex matter and one which shall be returned to later in this discussion. Here I shall explore some of the themes that shape and contribute to this lack of reciprocity.

Objectivity

Part of the more established models of professions, and one increasingly subject to critical comment, is the idea of objectivity. This complex term combines a number of themes. Questions of personal likes or dislikes on the part of the professional are not supposed to affect dealings with clients. Certain standardized procedures are brought to bear in order to assess the nature of the client's problems and to guide the conduct of the period of consultation. In some models this may mean that the professional is not concerned with the other as a whole person but only some aspect of the other; the process of consultation includes the negotiation and establishments of the particular rules of relevance of that professional encounter. It is not simply a question of how the professional defines the situation; the client is also concerned with objectivity and, indeed, may seek professional advice in preference to the less disinterested advice that might be offered by friends or family.

This theme of disinterested objectivity on the part of professional practice and the expectations of the client is, however, often quite vulnerable in practice. This is particularly the case with the 'caring' professions where issues of emotions and embodiment are especially to the fore. The literature has identified a variety of tensions between caring and objectivity or, perhaps in some cases, between 'caring for' and 'caring about' (Hugman 2005; Macdonald 1995). These questions are often sharpened when issues of gender and patriarchy are introduced into the analysis. This is partly a reminder of the fact that professional-client encounters are also gendered encounters and also of the argument that notions of objectivity and detachment, for long seen as the core of professional practice and identity, may represent a broadly masculine view of the world.

This idea of a tension between caring and objectivity is one of increasing importance and contributes, for example, to discussions about the dangers of 'burnout' and the dangers of becoming overinvolved in the painful or complex concerns of clients. In a sense there is another layer of objectivity placed on to the professional-client relationship, one which includes a recognition of these possible tensions and of the dangers of burnout and a failure to establish some break between professional work and life outside the hospital or consulting room. These debates are likely to continue but, from the point of view of this study, some element of distance is built into the professional-client relationship which is more than the unspoken and daily negotiated distances that we have consider elsewhere.

Surveillance and the professional gaze

A variation on these themes of objectivity and detachment, and one influenced by Foucaldian perspectives, is the idea of the professional gaze (Macdonald 1995: 175). In practice this may be identified as a series of different gazes, the medical, the legal, the financial and so on. The professional gaze is seen here as a particular combination of the specialized knowledge that the professional claims together with the positions of power assumed by or ascribed to the professional. In this manner, the individual client is shaped in a particular way, according to the relevances established prior to a particular professional encounter. We should not assume that this gaze is purely one-way although we know less of the client's gaze, of the ways in which the professional may be constructed according to the client's set of relevances. This consideration has increasing importance as more specialized knowledge and interpretations becomes available to the client through the media and the Internet. Despite this it would be safe to assume that the professional gaze, however modified, still contributes to a degree of asymmetry in the consultation.

Autonomy

Part of the process of professionalization over, in some cases, many decades, has been the claim for autonomy on the part of particular bodies of professionals. This process of social closure includes the claim to exclusive rights to control entry, to decide on programmes of accreditation and to maintain internal practices of discipline and sanctioning. A measure of professional power is the extent to which these claims are successful. However, the claims may not be invulnerable and may, increasingly, be the subject of media campaigns and state intervention.

What this means for the present discussion is that when clients approach professionals they do not simply approach another individual. The other is approached as a member of a particular professional body which is subject to regulations and practices that are frequently invisible to the client. Despite the growth of client-based pressure groups, the reverse is rarely the case and this is part of the imbalance in professional-client relationships. This structural difference between professionals and clients is emphasized in various forms of group practices and processes whereby clients may be passed on to other professionals.

Knowledge

I have argued throughout this book that knowledge, however partial and incomplete, is a key to understanding the idea of acquaintanceship. It has also been argued that this is a key element of professional-client relationships. But, what kinds of knowledge? And to what extent do these knowledges overlap?

At a first glance it might seem that the knowledge that professionals have, and which is part of the definition of the term 'professional', is very different from the kind of knowledge we are talking about when defining acquaintanceship. The former, as we have seen, is an accumulated body of specialized knowledge and understanding, which is the basis of sometimes long periods of training. The trainee professional is expected to acquire particular specialized knowledge and skills and to learn how to apply these and to demonstrate this acquisition through the internal processes of accreditation. A certain degree of abstraction also characterizes this knowledge in that it derives from general principles rather than the particularities of any one individual.

The abstraction and the formalized training attached to much professional education is clearly different from the kinds of knowledge that we are talking about in discussing acquaintanceship. It is, however, similar in that it is partial when it is applied to a particular client. Both acquaintances and professionals construct, through partial evidence and frameworks of interpretation, a biography of the other. But in the case of the professional this biography is constructed formally in terms of a medical record or case history, which can be referred to prior to each encounter. Further, again unlike acquaintanceship, this knowledge is not usually reciprocated. While the knowledge that a client has of a professional is rather similar to any kind of acquaintanceship knowledge, the knowledge that the professional has of a client is much more formalized.

Heath provides an illuminating discussion of the process by which the immediate knowledge that a doctor has of a patient is obtained and deployed. In a first interview, the doctor is more likely to open with questions establishing the patient's identity: 'It's Danny Fox, isn't it?' Having made a link between the patient and any available medical records the doctor will then ask something along the lines of 'what can we do for you today?' On a first encounter, the doctor will hardly ever ask 'how are you?' since this is likely to be confused with a conventional opening greeting that might take place between any acquaintances. However, this question might be asked on subsequent encounters since it will be more likely to be heard as part of an ongoing sequence of providing information about a medical condition (Heath 1981).

In the course of a consultation, a professional will build up a particular biography of a client. This biography might contain material which is closer to the partial fragments of knowledge that might be established between other sets of acquaintances: marital status, number of children, occupation, and so on. But these pieces of knowledge might be treated in a way that is different from the knowledge between acquaintances and assessed in terms of the overall rationale of the professional encounter. There are also the fragments of

60 Acquaintances

information that are 'given off' by the client, outside the more formal verbal exchanges such as bodily demeanour or style of dress. Knowledge obtained through a series of consultations might lead to the placing of the client according to a series of typifications, such as 'difficult client', which might be part of the wider professional subculture.

There is also another aspect of this professional knowledge and that is what Hughes (1971) refers to as 'guilty' knowledge. Put another way, there is often a kind of intimacy in the knowledge that a professional has of a client, bodily or emotional. Thus a professional may gain knowledge about the client's sexuality, general physical or mental health, marriage or bank balance. But this intimate knowledge still remains partial and does not make the professional encounter an overall intimate relationship although it does clearly distinguish it from relationships between strangers.

Confidentiality

We have seen that the knowledge that a professional has of a client is often partial, based upon specialized and more abstract training, formally recorded and build up over time and sometimes contains some intimate or 'guilty' secrets. As a necessary accompaniment to this there is a stress on confidentiality. There are legal and other limitations to this confidentiality but it is an important part of any professional code of practice and the expectation of confidentiality is part of the reason why a client goes to a professional in the first place. The knowledge may be shared with other professionals and may be sometimes written up as cases to be published but there are formal limits to, for example, the extent to which a professional may gossip about clients to other non-professionals. While confidences may be exchanged between acquaintances (and especially between other intimates) the guarantees and sanctions are normally much less strong. Indeed there may be a freedom to gossip about acquaintances (often based upon casual hints or impressions rather than a deliberate exchange of confidences) which may be limited in relationships between intimates.

All these features in different combinations enter into the professional consultation. Taken together they contribute to the asymmetrical character of this encounter and another way of expressing this is to point to a power differential between the professional and the client. Such a power differential may map on to other social divisions such as those in terms of gender or social class. Even recognizing that the power does not simply go one way it remains the case that the professional remains the dominant party. The whole consultation process, including the patterns of questions and answers, the process by which the client enters the consulting room and the symbolic and physical layout of the room itself serve as reminders that we are dealing with an asymmetrical mode of acquaintanceship.

Intimacy and distance in professional/client relationships

A theme running through this book is the idea of a balance between closeness and distance that is struck up in relationships between acquaintances. To a very large extent such a balance is tacit, negotiated and built up over time. Within the professional-client relationship this balance is the subject of more explicit elaboration and is stressed in some of the writings on professionals: 'The point is that relationships of professional caring combine intimacy with a degree of social distance' (Hugman 2005: 79). Hugman elsewhere refers to: 'issues of power, authority and responsibility that are not the same if done by a relative or friend' (p. 25).

Issues of imbalances of power, in all their complexities, are frequently discussed in close and detailed studies of consultations: 'Thus, from the very beginning of the interview, the doctor is typically in the initiating and the patient in the responding role' (Coulthard and Ashby 1976: 77). This is clearly illustrated in Heath's analysis, based on a considerable database of video-taped recordings (Heath 1981). There is a clear difference in the use and understanding of time (an important signifier of power imbalances) to doctors and patients: 'In over a thousand cases observed by Davis and Strong, only once did a patient end the meeting and not the doctor' (Strong 1977: 45).

Discussions of power imbalances and other tensions within the doctor-patient relationship have gained from the input from feminist scholars. As we have seen, feminist scholars have been in the forefront in exploring the meaning of care (Morgan 1996: 95–112). To what extent are there links between the paid care provided by professionals and the unpaid care provided by partners or family members? To what extent are there tensions between caring about and caring for in professional-client relationships and how are these managed? These issues have been given extensive treatment linking the day-to-day practicalities of care with wider ethical discussions.

Feminist-inspired studies have also focussed in particular on issues of emotions and emotional labour. The importance of the management of emotions, in others and in oneself, has been explored over a wide range of occupations, most professional or aspiring to professional status. The more recent developments in thinking about 'emotional intelligence' may have particular relevance in talking about the training of professions and the nature, or limitations, or professional expertise (Hugman 2005).

Another theme that has been introduced into the consideration is that of 'relationality' (Smart 2007). While this idea has a more general applicability it does have a particular resonance when talking about the ethics of care (Hugman 2005: 67–83). The emphasis is not simply upon the knowledge or the expertise of the professional or the needs and characteristics of the client but on the actual relationship between the two. Such an understand does not necessarily overcome the built-in tension between intimacy and distance but it does place it in a new light and open up a degree of reflexivity on the part of the professional and, indeed, the client.

What these discussions of care, emotion and relationality might contribute to the discussion of professional-client encounters is a shift in the weight of interest from the former to the latter. There is the danger that much of the discussion so far has given the impression of the client or patient as being simply at the receiving end of a particular sequence of encounters. There are, however, several ways in which this perspective may be limited:

- Clients and patients have to 'work' at being clients and patients and are required to cooperate in the professional encounters within which they may be involved.
- Clients and patients may make a point of seeking and acquiring some knowledge about their concerns, perhaps through the Internet or other readily available sources of information.
- Clients/patients are not social isolates but may exchange experiences of professional encounters with other friends, family members or acquaintances (Webb and Stimson 1976). Differences have been observed between the stories that patients may tell of their encounters (in which they may appear in a more proactive light) and actual observations of these interviews (Webb and Stimson 1976). This is not, from our point of view, a sign that these accounts are 'false' or self-serving. These stories have their own validity as stories and themselves frequently enter into and form the material of ongoing relationships of acquaintanceship or friendship away from the professional encounter.
- There are differences between cultural or economic contexts (such as between the US and the UK). These differences include the extent to which fees enter the consultation, the extent to which the client is able to 'shop around' or seek second opinions and, possibly, the degree of deference or otherwise shown by the patient to the doctor.

While increasing consideration of the client perspective within the professional consultation is vital to understanding the full relational character of this encounter it does not seriously undermine this requirement for some balance between closeness and distance and for this to be built into this encounter in ways which are more specific than we find in other patterns of acquaintanceship. There are, however, some further necessary modifications to this account of the professional-client consultation.

The consultation: further elaborations

I have argued that the consultation is at the core of the professional-client encounter and that it is here that we see both differences between and overlaps with these encounters and relationships between acquaintances. However, it will be noted that the discussion so far has been dominated by one particular form of encounter, that between a patient and a physician. To some extent this reflects the overall literature on professional-client relationships which is strongly weighted in the direction of doctor-patient encounters.

In other professional encounters, however, we may find important differences. In encounters between solicitors and clients, for example, the latter are more likely to set the objectives of the consultation and the role of the professional is more one of translating these objectives into a legal framework (Cain, 1983). It is likely that much of this will be paralleled in dealings with accountants or architects. The differences between these encounters and medical encounters will partly reflect (at least in the UK) the fact that the client is more likely to be required to pay a fee in these non-medical consultations. But they also reflect a lingering 'charisma of office' that attaches to the physician, a realization that matters of, literally, life or death may be at stake.

Even within the overall context of medical practice, the consultation between physician and patient is only one encounter among several. There are also, usually briefer, encounters with other health professionals such as nurses or pharmacists. There may also be encounters with alternative or complementary therapists. Here the consultations may be longer in duration and will almost certainly involve the payment of a fee. Despite the fact that some clients seek alternative therapies as part of a rejection of a medical model, the actual consultation may have some affinities with more established medical encounters (Bury and Gabe 2004; Lupton 2003). There will be the imbalances in terms of knowledge (albeit of a different kind) and perceived expertise. There will be the accumulation of knowledge by the therapist over time and this knowledge will not only be general (accumulated through training and experience) but also specific, relating to repeated encounters with a particular client. The greater length of these encounters may allow for the accumulation of more of this kind of specific, acquaintance, knowledge.

If we move beyond the medical consultation (but still remaining within the broad field of health care) it will be recognized that the encounter with the physician is only one of a set of possible encounters that might be sequenced. Thus a trip to a GP may be followed by a trip to the local hospital to get a blood test and both these encounters will also be accompanied by brief exchanges with receptions and, possibly, other patients. If we include periods of time in hospital, then the opportunities for developing acquaintances are multiplied considerably. Fairhurst's experience on an orthopaedic ward illustrates this sense of a sequence of fleeting acquaintances: 'Soon after entering the ward, ward personnel introduced themselves to me [using first names] as they passed by' (Fairhurst 1977: 164). Firth, similarly, describes her experiences in a tropical diseases hospital: 'We are quite an amicable little quartet in our ward; little overt communication, but there are clear signs of regard for others who are quickly "warned" if they are doing something palpably "wrong"' (Firth 1977: 145). This quotation provides a beautiful illustration of acquaintanceship at its most positive; the balance between distance and closeness does not remove the possibility for some mutual concern.

Conclusion

I am here beginning to stray beyond the consultation, which I see as being at the heart of many professional encounters. This is inevitable, given my particular interest in acquaintanceship, which has given rise to this chapter. Within the whole field of professional and near-professional encounters we have fleeting acquaintances, passing acquaintances (regular visits to a chemist, for example), work relationships (e.g. between professionals) and experiences within total institutions. All these, as we have seen, involve different kinds and dimensions of acquaintanceship.

Yet, there is some purpose in retaining a focus on the consultation as the core of this chapter since it raises particular considerations in the study of acquaintanceship. The consultation is normally arranged in advance at a specific time and in a specific place. Similarly, the consultation is limited in terms of time. The consultation has a certain lack of reciprocity built into it. This is partly in terms of the factors considered earlier in this chapter: differences in terms of knowledge, professional training and codes of ethics. But it is also in terms of something much more obvious: to the professional, the client is one of many whereas to the client the professional is distinct. This distinguishes the professional encounter from relationships between neighbours or workmates although not from relationships with taxi drivers or waiters.

Why are such encounters important in the study of acquaintanceship? In the first place, they are important in everyday lives in a modern society. Few people pass though their lives without some experiences of consultations and for some of these such encounters may be fateful, a source of anxiety and emotional intensity. Yet, for the most part, they retain the character of acquaintanceship rather than intimacy, even where intimate matters may be at stake.

In the second place they provide further illumination of the tension that is central to acquaintanceship; the tension between closeness and distance. This may reflect the case that highly personal issues – the state of one's marriage, bank balance or body – may constitute the topic of the consultation. Hence, the codes of professional ethics or the publicly or privately expressed concerns about over-involvement or burnout on the part of the professionals. More recent emphases on the importance of a more holistic approach on the part of the physician, which is not simply seeing the patient in terms of a set of symptoms, might intensify this tension (Nettleton 1995: 157).

Yet, these tensions, although formalized in codes of professional conduct or discussions between peers, highlight dilemmas that are common to the whole range of acquaintance relationships. What kind of knowledge do we have of our neighbours or workmates and what uses do we make of it? How far should we get involved in the concerns of others who simply happen to live next to us or work in the same office or who even pass us by each day? Professional encounters and consultations have their distinctive character but they can also illuminate aspects much closer to home and to the flow of everyday experience.

There is one further conclusion that might be drawn from this discussion. While the available literature tends to present these encounters from the point of view of the professional, there have been numerous forces at work to ensure that the client's perspective is also heard. This may be the consequence of state intervention and monitoring or it may be the consequence of the development of self-help groups among the clients themselves. There is, in addition, a growing body of literature seeing medical encounters from the point of view of the patients, or at least some of the more articulate ones (e.g. Davis and Horobin 1977). The theme of acquaintanceship may contribute to this shift of perspective and cause us to enquire into the knowledge that clients have of the professionals whose help they seek.

5 Passing acquaintances: overlapping timetables

Introduction

Chapter 2 dealt with overlapping spaces; the ways in which people find that they are living close or next to each other. In this chapter I look at overlaps in time. Here I am looking at the kinds of acquaintances that arise out of the fact that individuals have overlapping timetables and therefore find themselves, however briefly, in the same place and at the same time as other individuals. The difference, of course, is one of emphasis; neighbours, for example, overlap in terms of both time and space.

In previous chapters I was dealing with an identifiable and well-established body of literature but the same cannot be said for the issues that I am dealing with here. There is, of course, an extensive literature dealing with time but this rarely extends to a discussion of passing acquaintances.

I make no apologies, therefore, for introducing the subject matter of this chapter with some brief autobiographical vignettes.

a) Towards the end of the 1990s I found myself making regular train journeys between Stoke-on-Trent and Manchester. I would frequently find that I had some spare time on my arrival at the station and would usually then go to the buffet for a cup of coffee. On such occasions I observed a man sitting in more or less the same place on each occasion. He was smartly dressed, balding and about in his early 60s. He spent most of the time reading *The Daily Telegraph* and my memory is of him concentrating on the sport pages, although that may be wrong. He occasionally exchanged some brief words with the people who served in the canteen. One thing seemed very clear; he was not interested in catching a train. I speculated that he was probably retired or redundant and that he came to the station for his breakfast rather than eating alone but this was just one among several possible narratives. One day he was not there and he was not there the next day or the day after. I remember feeling a faint sense of loss. Later, he did reappear but by that time I was no longer making such a regular journey.
b) Trains feature quite a bit in these autobiographical fragments. When I boarded my train I took the end carriage as I knew from experience that

this was less likely to fill up until the last stage of the journey. Regular train travellers, I now know, routinely adopt similar strategies. Again, there were some faces and individuals that became familiar although I did not speak to any of them or give any sign of recognition. There was the woman with an inflatable cushion who was asleep for most of the journey. There was another woman, sometimes accompanied by a man, who was almost certainly an academic, probably in the natural sciences. There was the group of computer buffs who got on at the next station, and so on. There was, then, a variety of faces that I expected to see on these trips although not always in the same combination.

c) In an earlier period of my life I sometimes took an early train on Monday mornings from Lancaster to Manchester. In the waiting room, I noticed three men who sat close to each other and chatted mostly, it seemed, about the weekend football matches. Yet, when they boarded the train, they did not sit together but continued the journey individually reading their newspapers.

d) When I was in my early teens, having started at grammar school, I regularly made the journey both ways on foot. The only alternative to this two-mile walk was a complex journey by bus and train. On my return journey, somewhere close to the bridge that crossed the railway line, an elderly (or so he seemed to me at that age) but sprightly man would pass me, calling out something like 'hello, young Morgan!' I had very little idea as to who this man was. He was not a neighbour but he knew my name. I assumed that he knew my father, possibly through the church or the Labour Party. These encounters did not happen everyday but with reasonable frequency, enough for me to notice when they no longer took place.

e) From time to time, when I was up fairly early in the morning, perhaps taking a short walk or waiting for a taxi, I saw a woman walking her two dogs. We greeted each other. Later, she introduced herself as 'the dog woman' when we met at a departmental gathering at Keele University.

f) An early recollection of my father. I was probably in my early teens. I remember looking out of my bedroom window one rather misty Autumn morning and seeing my father standing on the street corner in a state of some mild, frustrated agitation. I asked my mother what was going on. She was obviously rather embarrassed by these activities and explained that he was waiting for Mr Fuller to leave his house and to get well ahead of my father before he continued his journey on the way to the station. My father did not like conversing with this particular neighbour on the train to London, probably preferring to read his newspaper.

Clearly, these examples could be multiplied from my own experiences and from the experiences of others. They are also slightly different and raise different issues. In some cases there was some prior knowledge (not necessarily reciprocal) and some exchanges. In other cases, the 'other' existed within my field of vision and I have no way of knowing whether there was any reciprocity of perspectives. What they have in common is a certain sense of regularity and the fact that the participants are clearly not intimates. But they are not exactly strangers either or, if they are, they come into the category of 'known strangers'.

If I were writing fiction, several, if not all, of these vignettes would be a point of departure. They would not normally be allowed to stand on their own. Thus, a common format might begin with two unrelated people, perhaps a man and a woman, making the same train journey together. An unexpected delay leads to their opening up a conversation whereby they discover they have much in common and arrange to meet for a meal. And so on. The fictional message is that these encounters (consider the films *Strangers on a Train* or *Brief Encounter*) are beginnings. The sociological message is that such encounters have their own validity and exist in their own right.

The preconditions of such encounters are fairly straightforward. The context is a rationally ordered, largely urban, social structuring, which is dominated by clock time. Even those people, such as the retired, who might be expected to have greater freedom in these respects, frequently attest to the value of regularity and routine. Although the individuals in these encounters lead, in most respects, quite different or at least separate lives, their individual timetables contribute to these points of intersection. To this extent the encounters are not accidental meetings. Individual lives are structured by working arrangements and the consequent balances between work and domestic life, by transport timetables as well as by personal habit or preference. Dogs require walking but when they are taken for a walk depends upon their owners' work-related timetables. While some spatial commonalities are also essential, the central point of these meetings is to do with time and the overlapping of personal, but frequently externally structured, timetables.

The reason why these are not exactly meetings between strangers is that some measure of knowledge exists, or more accurately accrues over time, about the participants. I know that this man reads a particular newspaper, that this woman uses a train journey to catch up on some sleep, that this woman has two dogs. In some cases, this knowledge is reciprocated or perhaps flows in reverse. This man knows my family name even if I do not know him. In some cases, perhaps many, I have no knowledge as to whether anything is known about me to the other person involved. It is possible that I might be completely invisible to the others on the train or in the station buffet. Or possibly they have composed speculative stories about me. Either way, the stories are more like lightning sketches or caricatures than fully elaborated biographies.

Rhythms and regularities

I have indicated that a precondition for the development of this kind of acquaintance is the existence of regular timetables that overlap at certain points. While regularities and routines are certainly to be found in rural life, the emphasis here will be upon the development of urban timetables. The rhythms of rural life differ perhaps in their natural or seasonal determinants and in the fact that the people who participate are, if not always intimates, frequently more than passing acquaintances.

The rhythms of modern urban life, the different 'timescapes' (Adam 1998), are based on a variety of external features. The first is the dominance of 'clock time' which, as E.P. Thompson argued so memorably, can be seen as one of the key foundations of modern capitalism (Thompson 1967). The second, and clearly linked to the development of clock time is the organization of work around notions of the working day, constructions that also extend to leisure activities. This working day, of course, is not confined to the conventional 'nine to five' but may be modified to take on board shift work, flexi-time, and so on. A third consideration, again related to the other two, is the separation of home and work, which leads to the necessity for regular journeys back and forth between the two locations. All these considerations underline what Zerubavel (1981: xvii) calls the 'rational elements of temporal organization'.

The term 'timescape' is appropriate since it highlights the interdependence of time and space; people are at certain places for certain prescribed periods of time. Further, it underlines the complexities of these time patterns and the different ways in which they mesh together. Consider a fairly everyday activity such as attending a concert. The concert is advertised to start at a particular time in a particular place and this timing frequently reflects assumptions about the working and domestic timetables of the players and, especially, the members of the audience. The individual pieces in the concert are timed in order to constitute a programme of a fairly standard length, normally with an interval somewhere in the middle. Concerts may be a rich source of acquaintances especially among the season-ticket holders and this emphasizes the fact that different individuals, with time life-projects and timetables find themselves in the same place at a particular time in the evening.

Returning to employment-based routines, it is important to note that these routines also impact on those who are not necessarily engaged in paid employment. The work routines of hospitals, surgeries, schools and supermarkets impacts on patients, pupils and their parents, shoppers and so on. These considerations, part of the continuous developments of modern societies, provide the basis for complex strategies of planning and coordination within households. Children have to be got to school or to nurseries, which have clearly delineated opening hours, and these movements have to be coordinated with the parents' working schedules. There are, as a consequence, many opportunities for the timetables of different individuals to overlap although this will be modified by the extent to which the journeys are made on foot or by public transport or within private cars.

It can be argued that these complex coordinated rhythms are subject to considerable modification within late modernity for a variety of reasons. The continued use, especially in Britain, of the private car, is one influencing factor, reducing the possibility of passing acquaintanceship. Another is the development of new working practices such as flexi-time, shift work and round-the-clock shopping as well as, in the spheres of leisure, extended opening hours for pubs and restaurants. These developments do not necessarily eliminate the possibilities of acquaintanceship but they may limit the development of the kinds of passing acquaintances described at the beginning of this chapter.

This section has emphasized the way in which modern or late modern societies provide the context for overlapping timetables and the development of acquaintances. The point is not simply that these timetables overlap because of regularities in the working day or opening hours, but that it becomes highly likely that any contacts between unrelated persons, however regular, will be necessarily brief. However, it has already been suggested that such timetables are not all externally structured and that some are the outcome of individual decisions and practices. The retired, the unemployed and those on vacation who might be thought to have 'time on their hands' still frequently tend to observe regular practices. This may be a consequence of a lifetime of observing externally imposed rhythms or the continuing need to coordinate one's activities with those significant others who are employed. Or, it may be a consequence of advice concerning the benefits of structuring one's daily life in terms of generating or maintaining a sense of meaning, personal identity or ontological security.

Some types of passing acquaintance

The fellow traveller

I noted that several of my examples outlined at the beginning of this chapter concerned train travel. This may reflect my own preference for travelling on public transport but it would seem that such 'others' are closest to the pure type of passing acquaintance. Their appearance has an observable regularity and this regularity is almost inevitably structured by the rhythms of working life as well as the rail timetables. Even the absences – reflecting holidays or periods of leave – arise out of these patterns. The journeys are sufficiently short to inhibit the development of longer intimacies and crowded conditions may also have similar consequences. Even where interaction does not take place, these other individuals are more than strangers because of the knowledge, fleeting and partial though it certainly is, that develops. The fellow traveller becomes identified by certain markers that distinguish him or her from other passengers; sleeping with the aid of an inflatable cushion, a particular newspaper, or the unmistakable signs of someone involved in education, such as papers to mark.

There is, as Delanty has noted, an element of liminality about these congruences of time and space (Delanty 2003: 141–2). As well as commuter trains, Delanty also refers to airport lounges or the recent coffee-bar chains such as 'Starbucks'. The liminality refers to the state of being 'betwixt and between', of moving between locations such as home and work and being governed by the expectations of neither. Yet, such liminality does not mean emptiness or normlessness. Rather, the use of the term does suggest the possibility of creating a small micro-world between the more apparently anchored sites.

Moran writes of train travel in these terms: 'The train carriage has always brought people together in an awkward mix of tolerance and irritation, proximity and distance, kinship and anonymity' (Moran 2007: 22). This list of oppositions has some affinities with the ways in which I understand the idea of acquaintanceship, especially in the interplays between proximity and distance. However, Moran reminds us that train travel has a history and points to a contrast between the 'season-ticket holders' and the 'commuters' (p. 25). The contrast is between a group of middle-class men (usually) sharing a carriage on their way to work and engaged in conversation or shared activities such as completing crossword puzzles. This 'golden age' has almost disappeared as carriages with 'airline seating', or perhaps even designed to accommodate standing passengers, replace the individual carriages seating around ten individuals. The modern-day commuter may still have a season ticket but it is the identity of a commuter, someone moving between home and work in a more standardized and less comfortable manner, which dominates. The overcrowding of many commuter trains reduces the possibilities of the kind of interaction described by Moran even further. However, waiting periods prior to boarding a train might continue to provide the opportunity for acquaintances to develop. The buffet at Stoke station, described earlier in this chapter, frequently provided occasions when I saw, and sometimes spoke to, others who were recognized by or known to me.

These encounters are so frequent and so routinized as to be unworthy of comment. Yet these meetings, and the way in which they may enter conversations with others on later occasions, have their own significance and can be memorable in a small way. This is well expressed by Letherby and Reynolds in their recent examination of train travel: '[W]e were told of the pleasure and freedom of talking to a fellow passenger you will never see again, a stranger regarding whom have have no responsibilities, an interesting person you might otherwise not have met' (Letherby and Reynolds 2005: 130).

The regular

In the case of the fellow traveller, both parties are in motion, travelling to different destinations. In the case of the regular, at least one of the parties is more static. Regulars include people who repeatedly visit the same shop, café or pub at more or less the same time. They may be regular in terms of habits (choice of drink, choice of newspaper) as well as in terms of time. The notion of the regular also implies another, almost certainly an acquaintance, who defines the other as a regular. This may be a shopkeeper, someone serving or another customer.

While the regular may have people with whom he routinely has conversations and who might even be defined as friends, in many cases the exchanges might be briefer, confined to a greeting or a nod. Again there may be an unspoken etiquette of distance, of not encroaching on another's personal space unless there are contrary indications. Nevertheless the regular, once again, is not a stranger. He or (one suspects more rarely) she is clearly distinguishable from others who may regularly visit the same space and some limited knowledge about the other exists or can be the basis for further speculation. The regular, as an acquaintance, may be defined by his regularity: 'you could set your watch by him'.

As an example, I can provide a piece of autobiography. After my father died, I found myself looking through the card index he kept in place of an address book. This did not only include names, addresses and telephone numbers but also little pieces of biographical information, sometimes (alas!) written in shorthand. One of them read, after the individual's name and address: 'H in H. Acquaintance [crossed out] Friend now'. 'H in H' referred to the pub *The Hand in Hand* where my father most usually had a drink on a Saturday morning. By the time I became aware of the person in question he had almost certainly crossed the border from acquaintance to friend. He was no longer someone with whom there was a likelihood of an exchange of conversation; he was now someone who (with one or two other individuals) was actively sought out on entering the pub. It became increasingly likely that the hour or so spent in the pub would be spent in the company of the other person, discussing politics and religion (the other person was a high Tory and an Anglican, my father a Methodist and a socialist) or attempting a crossword. The fact that he had made the transition from acquaintance to friend was indicated by the fact that I was introduced to him (he subsequently took some interest in my career) and that he was invited, along with another *Hand in Hand* regular, to my parents' golden wedding celebrations.

The fact that this other person was reclassified as a friend does not affect the current discussion. My father regularly visited this particular pub at about the same time on a Saturday morning. He became noticed by others as he became aware of other regulars. My father accumulated a great deal of knowledge about these others, although few of them could ever be defined as friends. So and so worked for a national newspaper, another was an ex-policeman, a third had once been banned from this particular pub for a period, and so on. Presumably, these others also accumulated a certain amount of knowledge about my father; that Methodists were not necessarily teetotal, for example. We can conceive of little clusters of individuals (again, mostly men) united by little apart from their co-presence and fragments of knowledge.

Within the British context, clearly pubs frequently play an important role in the construction of regulars and the practice of standing at or close to the bar facilitates interaction and the development of acquaintanceship. Fox, in her ambitious study *Watching the English*, devotes a whole chapter to the pub, arguing that here, unusually, 'the sociability rule' applies and it is acceptable to strike up conversations with perfect strangers (Fox 2004: 89). Such encounters might be part of the process of becoming regulars, persons who see each other regularly but often, one assumes, only within this particular setting of the pub. The use of nicknames to define regulars both shows the degree of familiarity that develops between regulars but also the limits of this familiarity. Fox's discussion of the etiquette of pub talk also points to the kind of balance between closeness and distance that we discover elsewhere in this discussion. To the outsider, the talk may sometimes seem passionate, even aggressive and often demonstrating a kind of masculine competitiveness. But the underlying assumption is that nothing should be taken too seriously and a vigorous attack on another's views should not be taken as a violation of the self. As with Simmel's discussion of 'pure sociability', the emphasis is upon maintaining the flow of talk and exchange rather than defeating an opponent. This may also account for what Fox describes as the 'free association talk in pubs', where there is a movement between topics that takes place without any of the conventional signs that such a change is taking place. Sticking to the point or completing a logical argument is less important than maintaining the flow.

While Fox develops her analysis with reference to English pubs and the construction of a sense of 'Englishness', Cavan's account of American bars raises some similar issues (Cavan 1973). She argues that these public drinking places are 'open regions' where it is possible to engage in conversations with hitherto complete strangers. The relationships here are often one-off with little past and little future. The content is typically small talk. Nevertheless these fleeting and fluid contacts are not necessarily without significance.

Another quite different area where notions of regulars are important is the pinball scene, described by Sanders (1973). Here the contact with regulars is mediated through the pinball machines and the way in which the play is conducted. 'In getting to know a [pinball] machine, the player also gets to know those who regularly play It' (pp. 58–9). Yet these relationships are 'strictly situational and formal'; they have little resonance outside the pinball area itself. The knowledge that an individual has of a pinball acquaintance is in terms of the other's style of play and little else. However, this partiality and segmentation is part of what is implied by the term 'passing acquaintance'.

While there can be many sites where 'regulars' may be identified, it is probably not accidental that the ones mentioned here are associated with leisure. There is a minimal degree of compulsion involved in their attendance. These sites therefore can be contrasted with places of employment or other places (such as allotments, sports teams or amateur dramatic societies) where some degree of regularity, signifying commitment to shared goals, is part of the routine expectations.

Others

'Fellow travellers' and 'regulars' are probably the more important types of passing acquaintances but they do not exhaust the possibilities. There are other kinds of passing acquaintances that accompany the carrying out of 'errands' (Wenglinsky 1973). Errands themselves may vary in terms of degrees of regularity and some may be so infrequent as to be more relevant to discussing 'fleeting', rather than 'passing', acquaintances. Here I am referring to those errands which take place with some regularity and/or at more or less the same time during the day. 'Errands' are those tasks which are necessary for the maintenance of everyday life but which are (except in some limited cases) unpaid. Here I am talking about shopping trips (getting the morning paper or going to the Post Office, for example), dog-walking and visits to a barber or a hairdresser.

My mother, for example, shopped more or less on a daily basis. My parents never owned a car so the idea of the weekly shop was unknown although, certainly after we bought a refrigerator, daily trips were not strictly necessary. However, it is likely that the frequent fleeting social encounters were of some importance to her. On returning from such trips she would tell us of who she had met, the exchanges overheard in the butcher's shop (often involving a well-known local political figure) and other encounters. Few of these people she met could be described as 'friends' although my mother frequently knew their names.

I do not think that my mother's encounters and the subsequent telling or re-telling of the stories were all that unusual. One of my motives in embarking on this project was seeing little clusters of people in the area where I usually did my shopping or sometimes in a local supermarket. They were having conversations and their encounters were almost certainly unplanned, arising out of their embarking upon similar errands. For the most part, I assume, the people I saw would not describe each other as friends but these small encounters were not without their significance.

In addition to errands, and distinct from both the kind of commuting experiences described earlier and the practices of 'regulars', are various kinds of leisure activities. These include evening classes, cultural events, participating in sports, and so on. In some cases, these events generate the kinds of 'fleeting acquaintances' discussed in a later chapter. Yet others are closer, in some respects, to work relationships – participation in voluntary associations, for example. However, attendance at fitness centres, evening classes and, to some extent, a series of concerts can also be the source of passing acquaintances. For example, for a while I joined a centre which had a swimming pool and sometimes went for a swim before breakfast. There were several other people who adopted a similar pattern, perhaps using the equipment in the gymnasium or the pool. There was relatively little interaction during the actual activities themselves (although I did notice a couple of women in the pool who seemed to spend a lot of time talking at one end rather than swimming) but there were some brief exchanges in the changing rooms afterwards. On the whole there seemed to be a tacit understanding that, unlike some other leisure activities, the purpose was not to be defined in terms of sociability but in terms of more individualized projects to do with health, body size and shape, and so on. But nevertheless, the brief, routinized exchanges were also part of the whole activity. And the same is probably also true for people attending evening educational classes.

One particular further illustration might by provided by church attendance or other kinds of participations in religious practices. (I shall confine myself to church attendance while recognizing that other religious traditions may present different – and similar – observations). The first point to note is that religious organizations have and impose their own particular rhythms, daily, weekly, annually and seasonally (Zerubavel 1981). The second is that while functionally inclined external observers might stress the social aspects of these occasions, the overt purpose is presented in somewhat different terms as some kind of religious obligation. Thus although worshippers might exchange words or gossip before or after the service, such exchanges are less likely during the actual service itself. However, the presence (or absence) of other fellow worshippers with whom one has some degree of acquaintance might be noted. Church-going may involve intimate relations (family, friends, etc.) but it is also a likely source of acquaintanceship; those others who one meets, and expects to meet, on a regular but passing basis.

Hybrid sites

Few of the sites or situations that I have described are purely sites of passing acquaintances. In other words, they are sites or occasions where one meets such acquaintances but the others included might not be confined to these. Thus on the journey to work, I might encounter intimates; I will certainly encounter strangers, those who I simply notice but who quickly disappear from view and may never be seen again. But clearly, as has been noted on several occasions, there is considerable fluidity in these categorizations.

A nice example of a hybrid site is provided by Davina Cooper's analysis of 'Speakers' Corner' in Hyde Park, London. She describes this as a 'comedic public space', shaped by the 'constitution and interaction of regulars and strangers' (2006: 755). The 'regulars' are many of the speakers and some of the people who go regularly to listen to them and sometimes to heckle. In the course of going regularly to the Corner they come to recognize other regulars. At the same time, there are strangers, casual visitors or tourists, or people who briefly interrupt their journey to listen to and, hence, to participate in the spectacle. We may speculate a little and argue that regulars derive something of their character as regulars in contrast to the others whose participation is much more fleeting and less engaged. The fluid, transient mass of non-regulars sustain the regulars as water sustains bathers.

Conclusion

These encounters have their distinctive features. Central here is their regular or repeated character; they are part of and contribute to the rhythms of daily life (Lefebvre 2004; Zerubavel 1981). The length of these encounters and what takes place between the participants may, on the other hand, vary considerably. As elsewhere, it is possible to establish a kind of continuum of passing acquaintances ranging from the very brief encounter where there are no exchanges to the longer encounters where they may be several exchanges, such as those between regulars. Such variation may influence the overall significance of these acquaintances, indicated perhaps, by the extent to which they are woven into a person's narratives on other occasions, with other sets of people. In these more significant examples, prolonged or permanent absences, may be the subject of extended comment: 'Haven't seen the *Telegraph* reader for some time.'

Whatever the variations, these passing acquaintances do have characteristics in common with other acquaintances. They are based upon knowledge, which is enough to establish an identifiable individual but which remains partial and often unelaborated. In the case of acquaintances which are simply based upon visual recognition (a fellow commuter, for example) this partial knowledge may be established quite quickly but will remain fixed and confined to a few quick brush strokes. The slim woman with the lap-top, for example. In other cases, the knowledge may accumulate and be enlarged and enriched over a long period of repeated exchanges.

Nevertheless, these acquaintanceships still retain a sense of distance, even in the case of the more repeated exchanges. If this distance is not maintained, the acquaintance may become a friend. It is as if there is some tacit agreement to maintain the acquaintanceship at a certain level and this may be aided by the use of nicknames, a sense of non-seriousness or possibly some shared activities such as solving crossword puzzles.

To what extent are such acquaintances, and the practices that go with them, gendered? To some extent, this discussion of passing acquaintances does, implicitly, play around with certain gendered oppositions such as public and private, outside and inside and so on. To meet passing acquaintances is to participate in spheres which might traditionally have been defined as masculine. Certainly some of the examples, especially those dealing with pubs and other arenas, have these connotations.

However, it is likely that this gendering of external public space has undergone considerable modification since the late 1980s although, as discussions to do with personal safety in public spaces clearly show, has not completely disappeared. Increasing female participation in the labour force also entails increasing participation in the public spaces that lie between home and work. Further, there have always been areas of public space (and hence the possibilities for generating acquaintances) which have been more open to women, as we see in the brief discussion of errands earlier. My tentative conclusion here (although this requires further analysis) is that while there is a gender dimension to acquaintanceship in general, in relation to passing acquaintances this gendering is relatively weak.

Another issue for consideration is to do with the possible 'Englishness' of this analysis. It could be maintained that the emphasis on distance implied by the word 'passing' does have particularly English connotations. Similarly, some of the locations for 'regulars' such as pubs, seem to be especially English; Kate Fox pays some attention to the etiquette of pub talk in her book on *Watching the English* (Fox 2004). She also notes the way in which distance is maintained on commuter trains, as if the passengers were terrified of observing anything beyond the normal rules governing behaviour in public places.

Against this we may note, as we have seen, that behaviour in American bars in some ways has similarities to English pubs, at least in terms of the availability of customers to more extended conversations. Further, Moran's brief references to the history of commuter travel in Britain (Moran 2006) suggest that the spatial organization of carriages and, possibly, social class also influence patterns of informal social interaction. Finally, it could be argued that the presence of passing acquaintances is a feature of all urbanized societies. Different cultures may do the passing differently, with more elaborate or longer patterns of interaction in some cases rather than another, but the acquaintances are still acquaintances, that is, people other than intimates or complete strangers.

What, then, is the significance of passing acquaintances? I have argued that these form a particular class of acquaintances characterized by related limited knowledge and relatively limited interaction, although both these dimensions can vary considerably. What they have in common is the fact that their occurrence is structured by timetables, personal and institutional. The knowledge that the parties have of each other will be, as in other cases, partial but accumulated, often slowly, over time through repeated encounters.

As with other kinds of acquaintance, some of these people encountered on a daily or weekly basis in the course of following everyday routines may cross the border and become intimates: friends, partners or lovers. But the majority will remain as acquaintances and their significance is not to be limited to their being a possible source of closer relationships. Further, there may be some instrumentality in these passing acquaintances. Pubs can be sites of all kinds of informal trading, legal and illegal. Further, the regulars in pubs and other sites may be part of loose networks that provide local knowledge and local contacts, useful when looking for joiners, painters and decorators, piano tuners or gardeners. This is part of the 'strength of weak ties' argument (Grannoveter 1973) and should not be overlooked.

However, I would not wish to limit the significance of passing acquaintances to their possible instrumental significance just as I would not wish to seem them simply as a source of some closer relationships. Again, we are dealing with a continuum here, ranging from the person seen every working day but with whom one exchanges few, if any, words, to the regulars in the pub, perhaps seen less frequently but with whom one may exchange more extended and more animated conversation, even if the relationship does not extend beyond the walls of the inn. I see such acquaintances, in all their variety, as important in the construction of everyday life.

Everyday life itself is a complex term and has several dimensions (Morgan 2004). I am referring here to those regularities and repetitions that are hardly worth talking about. ('Where have you been?' 'Nowhere'. 'Who did you see?' 'Nobody'). The importance of temporal routines has been noted by several authors (e.g. Zerubavel 1981). However, the stress here is frequently on the routines themselves rather than the others encountered in the process of following these routines. But it is these together, the routines and the others encountered, that go to make up a sense of normality and the everyday. To this extent they are part of the construction of a moral order.

In order to explore this further, consider the word 'regular'. In this chapter I have used it as a noun. While the word, in an English context, refers to a regular visitor to a pub it could also be extended to the other kinds of acquaintances mentioned in this chapter; the fellow commuter, the joggers, the dog-walkers, the concert-goers. But it is also frequently used as an adjective and here we encounter the moral connotations. To be regular in one's habits is to be disciplined and reliable if, sometimes, also a little boring. The phrase 'a regular guy' implies this and more, someone who is morally trustworthy. Clearly, I have little opportunity of really knowing the moral character of the person I see walking the dog every morning. Nevertheless, some of these wider connotations might cling to the passing acquaintances. They provide reminders of a regular and ordered world (perhaps contrary to the world I hear about on the radio before leaving the house) part of everyday reality itself (Berger and Luckmann 1967). It is not so much the moral character (about which I know little) of the individuals encountered on a day-to-day basis; it is the fact that these encounters take place regularly and unspectacularly that is of significance.

6 Fleeting acquaintances *in* time *and* space

Introduction

In the previous chapter I considered what I call 'passing acquaintances', those others who might be encountered on a fairly regular basis but where the actual interaction is brief and contained. To simplify, these acquaintances arise out of overlapping timetables. In this chapter I consider those acquaintances that may be equally short lived (although not necessarily so) but which are rarely, if ever, repeated. I have in mind here encounters with shop assistants, waiters and waitresses and taxi drivers as well as encounters in coffee houses, clubs, pubs and other places associated with entertainment or sociability.

It may be thought that these examples lie at the very fringe of, or even beyond, what might be understood to be acquaintances. Especially in a modern urban environment such encounters may be extremely frequent and easily forgotten. Names can rarely be attached to individuals encountered in this way and the knowledge acquired is frequently very partial and possibly erroneous. However, these individuals are still more than strangers and certainly more than the strangers one might pass in the street on one's way to a cafe or a department store. Unlike these other strangers they have a degree of fixity and they are not anonymous to the extent that they become completely interchangeable.

I discuss these fleeting encounters under a variety of headings, designed to show the ways in which an analysis of these meetings may contribute to our general understanding of acquaintanceship:

1 The encounters are rule governed.
2 The encounters involve some acquisition of knowledge of the other.
3 The encounters are structured by the spatial and temporal arrangements of urban life.
4 The encounters have a significance over and above any initial instrumentalities.

Rules of fleeting acquaintances

Some London clubs have a members' table in their dining rooms. This is where members, who have no pre-arranging dining companions and who do not wish to dine alone, may sit, joining whoever happens to be sitting at that table. They are obliged to join that member or those members and to engage in conversation; other members may join them later. Members are not obliged to remain at the table once they have completed their meal. These practices have a long history. Similar rule-governed interactions between former strangers are recorded as taking place in the London coffee houses of the eighteenth century: 'distinctions of rank were temporarily suspended; anyone sitting in the coffee house had a right to talk to anyone else, to enter into any conversation, whether he knew the other people of not, whether he was bidden to speak or not' (Sennett 1974: 81). There are some overlaps here with our discussion of pubs and bars presented in the previous chapter. Any differences are differences of emphasis. In discussing regulars I am concerned with repeated and reasonably regular encounters. In the case of the London clubs or eighteenth-century coffee houses, such encounters may be repeated (indeed, they may take place between intimates) but, equally, the participants may never encounter each other again.

Closer to our own times, similar obligations to engage in conversation with hitherto strangers would seem to apply at dinner parties of varying degrees of formality. Those attending academic conferences (and identified as such through wearing badges) may also feel a license, if not an obligation, to enter into conversation with other, previously unknown, delegates encountered at breakfast, coffee breaks or on some other informal context.

Even within the short list of structured encounters we can see a considerable variety in the rules and their application. The conference delegate probably has more leeway or latitude than the person sitting at the member's table or entering an eighteenth-century coffee house. Nevertheless these practices have some similarities. The first is the obligation or the license to enter into conversation with the other, thus enlarging one's knowledge of the other. The second is that the other may be a complete stranger although this is not always necessarily the case. Further, there is no guarantee that the acquaintanceship will continue beyond the particular framework, limited in time and space.

However, these kinds of encounters do not necessarily serve as models for all fleeting encounters. In all these cited cases, the social field from which the acquaintances are drawn are clearly limited, often severely so. The members of the London club are elected and are required to pay an annual fee; they normally come from a relatively limited range of class or status group backgrounds. A narrowly defined group of professionals constitutes the conference delegates while the dinner guests share some relationship with their host or hostess. One assumes that similar informal limitations structured the London coffee houses, perhaps even before an individual entered the door. This social limitation means that a lot is shared even before the conversation begins. The degrees of separation between any two acquaintances of this kind will be relatively few.

It will be argued that these relatively structured sets of expectations shaping relationships between acquaintances are not typical of the whole range of fleeting encounters. If these other, less formalized, encounters are rule governed, it might seem that the rules will often be similar to those governing encounters between strangers, such as the sets of expectations to do with distance and personal space, coordinating movement in public places, avoiding anything more than fleeting eye contact and so on. These kinds of rules have been well discussed in a variety of sources and are at the heart of much of Goffman's writings to do with encounters in public spaces (Goffman 1971).

While these rules are important they are not sufficient to define the nature of fleeting acquaintanceship as opposed to encounters between strangers. In the latter, the stranger remains the stranger; in the former, the stranger moves closer to being an acquaintance. In the cases that I am concerned with there is some intentionality on the part of the actors, not only to be in a particular place at a particular time, but also to encounters others. When we go into department stores or cafes we expect to encounter shop assistants and waiters or waitresses. When I hail a taxi, I expect to meet a taxi driver. In other cases, the expectation might be reasonable although the outcome is not inevitable. If I go to an art gallery I might expect to meet fellow art lovers although choice, personality and circumstances will determine whether these others move from strangers to acquaintances.

The rules that apply in connection to these kinds of fleeting encounters are various but can be classified under two broad headings, distinguished according to their level of generality:

- There are specific, although rarely articulated, rules governing the relationship between customers and service providers. These might be seen as the forms of etiquette and politeness that are routinely expected in such encounters. Although rarely written down, these rules become obvious once breached.
- There are the more general rules, which often inform (again rarely at an explicit level) these more specific encounters and which bring us back to the problem, encountered at several points in this analysis, of achieving some kind of balance between closeness and distance.

This talk of rules and of the distinctions between them, may provide an unrealistic sense of concreteness. We may find such rules outlined in books of etiquette (books that have informed much of Goffman's writings) but it is likely that they are learned more by observation or by more general understandings of how to conduct oneself in new or unfamiliar situations.

In the case of the former sets of rules, we are dealing with the structured expectations between customers and service providers and these are frequently the subject of discussion in newspapers and elsewhere. Complaints about the rudeness or lack of attention of shop assistants or others in similar positions are not uncommon and these are often paralleled by complaints about the rudeness of clients. This might suggest that these rules, for the most part unwritten and unspoken, become more obvious when they are breached. For example Ulla Forseth tells of the complaint of a bank teller about a customer at the head of the queue who insists on continuing to have a conversation on his mobile phone (Forseth 2005). Here it might be argued that the customer is guilty on two counts; failure to attend to the business at hand and failure to recognize the other as a person.

This indicates that these everyday fleeting encounters are often more complex than might at first be imagined. Some attention to the business at hand is required yet a single-minded attention might seem to be brusque and off-hand. Some recognition of the other as a person might reasonably be expected but this should not be at the expense of the more immediate concerns and should not dwell upon considerations that might be deemed irrelevant to the encounters; gender, sexuality, disability, ethnicity, and so on. Further, these delicate balances will vary according to the working environment and the structure of expectations on both sides. A certain amount of banter and flirtation might not be out of place in bars and restaurants but may not be acceptable elsewhere.

We can develop these complexities by referring to Wadel's useful discussion of the hidden work of everyday life (Wadel 1979). Clearly, the shop assistants, bar staff, bank tellers, etc. are engaged in work and this work includes varying degrees of emotional or aesthetic labour. But what is important to note is that the clients or customers are also engaging in work. To some extent, theirs is the more difficult task as a consequence of both the supposed decline of clear rules of etiquette and the rise of mass consumerism and consumers' participation in a wide range of services and leisure activities. Yet, customers and clients need to work at being customers and clients and this work also involves measure of emotional or aesthetic labour. In other words these encounters are collaborative (although not necessarily always wholly congruent) activities in which both parties are involved in forms of work.

One of the most fruitful developments in the sociology of work and occupations from the late 1980s has been the analysis of emotional, and more recently, aesthetic, labour. This has, in part, been a reflection of the development of a more gendered understanding of employment relations and of the significance of service occupations in modern economies (Hochschild 1983). One way of exploring emotional labour might be in terms of this kind of balance between attending to the business at hand while also recognizing the other as a person. I shall return to this theme in the conclusion but will develop it here with a simple illustration.

When I first arrived in Manchester in the 1960s, and for some time after, buses had both a driver and a conductor. The latter would collect fares and issue tickets, answer brief enquires about destinations and perhaps engage in some mild banter with the passengers. All this disappeared with the arrival of buses where the driver would collect fares from the passengers as they entered through the front door. Shortly after these new, labour-saving, buses were introduced passengers would begin to thank the driver on leaving the bus and the driver would reply with a 'see you' or something similar. Passengers and driver became the most fleeting of acquaintances, if that. Nevertheless, there seemed to be some unspoken desire to have something more than just a commercial transaction involving the provision of a service in exchange for a fare. What was interesting was how quickly this pattern developed without, as far as I was aware, any explicit demands being made of the customers faced with this, then, unfamiliar form of transport. Whether there is anything distinctively English about such evolving exchanges is a matter for further discussion (Fox 2004).

In comparison with the interaction between bus drivers and their fares, encounters in restaurants or department stores might seem much more elaborate and here the balance between the instrumental and the more expressive or human becomes even more complex. On the one hand, the service providers (the bank tellers or shop assistants) are employed in order to make successful sales. But they are also selling the reputation of the store or the restaurant or the bank as a kind of balance where customers and clients feel welcome and would wish to return. In addition, part of their job expectations include the positive gains expected when 'working with people' (Forseth 2005). There is clearly a strong element of impression management and performativity in their dealings with customers but, as has often been noted, pleasure may be gained from the successful accomplishment of such performances and from some measure of personal identification with the performance so that it does not simply remain on the surface.

From the point of view of the customers, they too have certain instrumental objectives although accounts of 'retail therapy' might suggest other considerations may also apply. There is, almost certainly, an expectation of some pleasurable encounters or, at least, the avoidance of any form of social discomfort. Such discomforts might be provided by the employee who seems too offhand or brusque. But equally, too obvious an engagement in putting on a performance on the part of the employee might also be a source of discomfort.

Yet employees have other customers to serve and customers have other errands to complete and so a delicate balance is aimed for between the business at hand and some measure of recognition of the other as more than a customer or a shop assistant. Achieving this balance is part of what is meant by emotional or aesthetic labour and this labour is performed by the customer as well as the employee. However, the employee has to engage in this work throughout the working day.

Another way of locating this balance is to see it in terms of the balance between distance and closeness, a balance that we have argued is part of the practices associated with acquaintanceship. The boozy client in Johnny Mercer's song, 'One For My Baby' recognizes that the bartender has to remain true to his code, i.e. to maintain some degree of distance from the sorrows of his customers. This also applies in some less structured encounters, i.e. those encounters (such as visits to art galleries, museums or concerts) where the strangers concerned are engaged upon a common activity and who have, one may presume not always accurately, some shared interest. The awkwardness of these kinds of encounters is well illustrated in Lofland's study, *Doomsday Cult* (Lofland 1966) in the section where the handful of original cult members are considering ways of recruiting new followers. Among these proselytizing strategies they included directly approaching people in museums and other public places. However, the difficulties of going up to strangers and saying something like 'that sure is an interesting bear' were recognized. There is some recognition of the way in which casual encounters in public places can be, or can be seen as, the opening moves in something more exploitative whether it be financial, sexual or, indeed, religious. Perhaps more 'genuine' encounters are to be found in sporting events where a sense of collective excitement or disappointment might reduce inhibitions and may provide a more legitimate basis for acquaintanceship, albeit often of a fleeting kind.

Knowledge and fleeting acquaintanceship

It is an argument running throughout this book that acquaintanceship is a form of knowledge and it is this form of knowledge that distinguishes it from relations between strangers or between intimates. Consider the knowledge that clients may gain about taxi drivers in even a relatively short journey. Over the years I have encountered taxi drivers who are (or who present themselves as) keen gardeners, active members of a choir, passionate about art, planning to go off to Cyprus or hoping to join the police force. Similarly, I have provided information about myself, relating to my ultimate destination, my work or the part of the country that I originally come from. Clearly, little of this knowledge is particularly intimate (thus observing the rules outlined above) and the encounter is constrained by the position of the customer behind the driver as well as by various external or internal background noises.

But this is not the whole story. Fred Davis, in his short article on the taxi driver and his fare (Davis 1959), notes how taxi drivers develop a series of typifications about their clients. Davis records the following: 'The Sport', 'The Blowhard' (a false Sport), 'The Businessman', 'The Lady Shopper' and the 'Live Ones'. These typifications are more than stereotypes based upon, say, assumed racial characteristics or age although these too may enter into their elaboration. They may be based upon how the customer is dressed and whether their manner indicates a familiarity or lack of familiarity with hailing cabs. It will certainly be based upon where the customer is picked up (a smart hotel, close to a red-light district, a fashionable department store) as well as what the customer is carrying. Thus there is an interplay between prior knowledge, built up over time and emerging out of interactions with other drivers and fares, and the immediate appearance of a particular client. On the basis of these typifications and the prior knowledge, the driver may be able to assess whether the fare will present any problems and the probable size of the tip.

One obvious feature about the example of the cab driver (and, indeed, of many of the encounters described in this chapter) is the asymmetrical character of the fleeting relationship. The customer may see just one or two cab drivers in the course of a day in town; the driver sees dozens of fares. This means that the urban worker (the cab driver, the traffic warden, the bartender) has a lot of cumulative experience to draw upon, experience which is mediated through and shaped through sharing experiences with other similar workers. Joel Richman, in his study of traffic wardens, shows how telling stories are an important part of this occupational subculture and that these stories can serve a variety of functions including initiating newcomers, developing a sense of solidarity and constructing members of the public (Richman 1983). This asymmetry is a feature of many such relationships in an urban environment and it is likely that similar knowledge and sets of typifications are deployed in a wide range of service occupations. On the whole sociology has concentrated more on occupational subcultures and hence we know more about this side of the encounter than about the perspectives of the clients or customers.

But, as we have seen, not all fleeting encounters are structured in this way, that is between a service provider and a client. As a way of characterizing other encounters we might return to the phrase 'fellow travellers', used in the previous chapter. There I was dealing with individuals who regularly made the same journey in the co-presence of the other. Here, I am talking about encounters which might sometimes be more intense but which do not have this quality of regularity or repeatedness. The possibility of striking up an acquaintance in the course of a shared journey is a staple feature of much fiction. Herman Melville's *The Confidence Man* (first published 1857) is about a whole series of fleeting acquaintanceships established and dropped in the course of a trip on a Mississippi steamer. These, for the most part, might be seen as 'genuine' fleeting acquaintances but most other fictional accounts see the initial fleeting acquaintance as leading to something more, most famously perhaps in the film *Brief Encounter*. Hitchcock's *Strangers on a Train* presents a more sinister account of these encounters.

Here I am concerned with those, for the most part, 'one off' encounters on public transport or in some other public site. There is a popular belief, supported by some anecdotal evidence, that these short-lived (at least in terms of the whole lifespan) encounters may sometimes have a particular form of intensity; the idea of pouring out all ones troubles to a complete stranger, secure in the knowledge that the encounter ends when one or both of the parties leaves the train or plane, is an appealing one. The following (reconstructed) account was provided by a friend:

> I had fastened my safety belt when I noticed that the young man next to me seemed to be in a state of some agitation. After some internal deliberation, I asked his if he was OK, wondering if he had some anxiety about flying. The young man revealed that he had just broken up with his girlfriend and spent much of the rest of the short flight in elaborating on his unhappiness.

From my own accounts I can recall a young woman anxious about what she will find when she visits a sick relative in hospital and another young woman who explained at some length the benefits of transactional analysis. A less 'serious' encounter involved a Scotsman who invited himself to complete the *Guardian* crossword with me.

It is clear that in these cases the kind of knowledge being deployed is different from the more structured encounters discussed earlier. We do not necessarily get a 'fully-rounded' picture of the person but we may gain some detailed knowledge of a particular facet of another person's life. These encounters are memorable because of their short-lived intensity. Even less dramatic encounters can provide knowledge which is more than simply categorical and this can often be rounded a little through prior understandings developed through shared (to some degree) cultural understandings.

In this discussion of the knowledge deployed in fleeting acquaintances we can see at least two types of knowledge being brought into play. The first is based upon sets of typifications developed over time through participation in both a particular occupational (or other) subculture and a 'wider' culture. This applies, for example, in the more instrumental encounters where employees develop typifications of clients and clients, similarly, develop some routine understandings of the employees. The second is the more idiosyncratic, if partial, information that is attached to a particular individual. This latter may also be divided into the more performative presentations of self and the more intimate revelations of an 'inner' self, remembering, of course, that it is frequently difficult to make clear distinctions here.

Contexts and sites

Throughout this chapter I have assumed, mostly implicitly, that these particular encounters are a feature of urban society. Indeed, the very idea of urban culture would seem to be very closely associated with fleeting acquaintances and this is part of a popular critique of urban society. However it is possible to think of exceptions. In a time of large-scale tourism, to ever more remote areas of the world, and globalized travel, fleeting acquaintances would similarly come to seem even more widespread. Tourists, and those with second homes, will be found in rural as well as in urban areas. Farmers, for example, may provide accommodation for tourists in order to supplement or to diversify their incomes in times of dwindling or uncertain returns for their more traditional activities (Brandth and Haugen 2005). Similarly, global travel will increase the possibilities of fleeting acquaintances in airports, planes, cruises and other sites associated with movement between continents.

It can be seen that the fleeting acquaintances developed in the course of travel and tourism are of two sorts. There are the asymmetrical kind where one party, normally a service provider, is more firmly anchored to a particular site or place and has their own network of friends, colleagues or close acquaintances. Seymour, for example, has explored what happens when children are brought up in hotels or guesthouses run by their parents (Seymour 2007). The customers, on the other hand, often, if not always, represent the fleeting acquaintances as do these providers to the clients themselves. But there are also the acquaintanceships (again of a fleeting nature often) that develop between the travellers or tourists themselves; the chance encounters in the airport lounge or on the tourist coach, plane or cruise ship. These encounters tend to be more symmetrical, as we find with fellow travellers.

We may argue, therefore, that globalization has increased the range of possibilities for fleeting acquaintances beyond the more familiar urban or metropolitan context. Nevertheless, it seems likely that these contexts will remain an important, if not a sole, site for such encounters and that the principles involved are more or less the same whether in urban or less urban settings. The already discussed distinction between the more asymmetrical kind of acquaintanceship between service providers and clients/customers on the one hand and the more symmetrical versions between fellow travellers or customers applies in both cases, for example.

There are still good reasons why we should concentrate on the urban context in this discussion of fleeting acquaintances. First, there is the increasing complex and varied division of labour which characterizes city life. The richness of these divisions of specialized skills and services is well described by Walter Benjamin:

> In the arcades, one comes upon types of collar studs for which we no longer know the corresponding collars and shirts. If a shoemakers shop should be neighbor to a confectioner's, then his festoons of bootlaces will resemble rolls of licorice. Over stamps and letterboxes roll balls of string and of silk. Naked puppet bodies with bald heads wait for hairpieces and attire.
>
> (Walter Benjamin from *The Arcades Project*, in Bridge and Watson 2002: 394)

What needs to be remembered is that this surrealist juxtaposition of items reflects and conceals loose networks of craftsmen and women, shop-keepers and occasional customers with equally specialized knowledge and interests. These highly specialized activities, together with the more standardized activities of department stores and everything in between, make up the complex divisions of labour that characterize urban settings and which make cities such a rich source of, largely asymmetrical, acquaintances.

The other important feature of urban life, partly connected to and indeed part of this complex division of labour, is the systems of transportation and the modes of interconnection. Cities are defined and symbolized by their metro systems, their urban bus routes, their streets, avenues, alleys and short cuts. These systems facilitate the commuter, the tourist, the day trippers and the *flaneurs*. Many of these will be and will remain strangers to each other as they pass in the street or the entrance to the subway. But there will also be fleeting exchanges of conversation between people who temporarily share the same space at the same time. Or there may be simply visual, often asymmetrical recognition as when we recognize a well-known eccentric or 'character' or when the *flaneur* accumulates visual impressions of others in the course of his perambulations.

One further aspect of city life, especially relevant to our purposes is the existence of recognized places of public assembly. Some of these will be provided by the state or commercial organizations for specific purposes such as sports stadia, large concert halls or other public places. But the more important will be the parks, the squares, the boulevards where people parade, demonstrate or arrange to meet each other. An illustration of this kind of public site is provided by this description of Parque Central in San Jose, the capital city of Costa Rica: 'Parque Central remains a vibrant center of traditional Costa Rican culture and is inhabited by a variety of largely male workers, pensioners, preachers and healers, tourists, shoppers, sex workers, and people who just want to sit and watch the action' (Low 2002: 357). With suitable variations, every city could provide one or more example of this kind of location. Such sites have been, and remain, sites of contestation around the right to assemble and to demonstrate, between different classes or interests such as those between the 'rough' and the 'respectable' or between commercial interests and more diffuse public expectations. From our point of view, they are also sites for the development of fleeting acquaintances.

There is one further aspect of city life which is worth mentioning in this context. This is the way in which modern cities have blurred the distinction between day and night (Melbin 1987) as witnessed by accounts of the 'night-time economy' or the '24/7' city. Clearly much of this development is associated with leisure, consumption and entertainment and with the growth of bars, clubs and restaurants that stay open through the night. These developments multiply the opportunities for fleeting acquaintances, embodied, short-lived but often, in some small ways, memorable. Their location (for the customers at least) outside daily routines enhances, perhaps, the possibilities that these encounters, although fleeting, will be remembered.

Here, as elsewhere in this discussion, we have a clear division between the service providers and the clients or customers. The former remain in one place for given periods of time and have their own informal networks of varying degrees of intensity but other than fleeting. The latter are there less frequently and have different kinds of commitments to the site in question. The clients will normally be fleeting acquaintances (if that) as will many of their fellow customers or participants in the night-time scene. And here, again as elsewhere, we have a distinction between the 'insiders' and 'the outsiders', perhaps a more fluid version of the distinction between locals and cosmopolitans. The insiders are the employees, together with some regulars and intimates. The outsiders are the visitors and customers, although some of them may wish to give the impression of being insiders.

All this is a reminder that these urban sites are (as with the case of Hyde Park Corner discussed in the previous chapter) hybrid sites, made up of insiders and outsiders, fellow travellers and regulars, strangers, intimates and acquaintances both passing and fleeting. If we are concentrating on fleeting acquaintances in this chapter it is with a full recognition of the fluidity of these boundaries but also arguing for the particular close association between urban life and culture and fleeting acquaintances.

Significance of these encounters

I have argued that, typically, these fleeting encounters take place in urban contexts although they can also be seen as part of global travel and tourism. Perceptions of urban life tend to be polarized between the romantic and the negative (Bridge and Watson 2002) and fleeting acquaintances play a part in both sets of images. The more romantic vision tends to celebrate the fluidity, the diversity and the endless possibilities of urban life. Here the fleeting encounters, conversations in bars or shops or the numerous opportunities to observe and to absorb are the tangible, embodied representations of this diversity and richness. Within the more negative accounts, on the other hand, the fleeting acquaintances merge with strangers and convey a sense of an order which gives little recognition to individual personalities. The fluidity and the movement become an impersonal rush, an ever-present threat. The 'others' are either merged into a mass or, alternatively, seen as isolates, whether in a crowd or on their own. The title of Riesman's influential book seems to sum it up: *The Lonely Crowd* (1961). Sometimes the emphasis may be on 'the lonely', sometimes 'the crowd'; the one a reflection of the other.

Perhaps the fact that there are such different ways of understanding urban life and culture is yet further indication of the fluidity of that culture itself. The same set of experiences and observations can be understood in different ways. Consider one of the most celebrated representations of urban life, Edward Hopper's *Nighthawks* painted in 1942. As most readers will remember, the painting consists of a café or diner, late at night. The curved glass serves as a barrier between the observer and the dark empty street outside. Inside are three customers and a man in a white jacket and cap who is serving.

Hopper is quoted, in relation to this painting: '*Nighthawks* seems to be the way I think of a night street. I didn't see it as particularly lonely. I simplified the scene a great deal and made the restaurant bigger. Unconsciously, probably, I was painting the loneliness of a large city' (quoted in Renner 1990). This suggests that the painting can be seen as representing loneliness and alienation (although Hopper himself does not seem to fully endorse this view); certainly it has often been seen in this way. But even a casual glance at the painting suggests that other things may be going on. The man and the woman, although not looking at each other, are clearly acquainted and possibly intimate. They may or may not be in the middle of a conversation with the man who is serving. They may be regulars, or they may have just dropped in. They contrast with the third customer, the man with his back to the street and to us, the viewers. He seems to be truly an isolate. But in an odd way he seems to be at home in that setting, his arms resting on the bar. He too may be a regular.

Clearly, we cannot know the answers to these questions but part of the appeal of Hopper's paintings is the sense that they suggest the possibilities of stories and continuities beyond the particular compositions. If, as I have suggested elsewhere (Morgan 2005, 2008) we can seen communities as nexuses of stories, we may also see much of urban life as a series of possible stories.

Jane Jacobs, as we have seen in the previous chapter, celebrates much of urban life as a source of passing acquaintances and, in common with many other commentators, provides the clear link between cites and strangers: 'cities are, by definition, full of strangers. To any one person, strangers are far more common in big cities than acquaintances' (Jacobs 1969[1961]: 30). Yet she also recognizes the fluidity of these distinctions and an initial stranger may become a passing acquaintance and, possibly, even an intimate. Much, of course, depends on how you define 'stranger'. To me, part of the definition of stranger includes some kind of sense of interchangeability. For example, I look out of my window and see a group of young people, I assume students, kicking a ball around. To a large extent these young people, seen at a distance, are more or less interchangeable with any other group of young people engaged in a similar activity. If pushed, I could probably say how many students there were and give some brief account according to very general categories; gender, presumed ethnicity, age, and so on. But they are, like many people I see when moving around the city, strangers.

Contrast this, with someone who serves me in a department store. There may be some brief exchanges about the quality of the goods being purchased, advice about maintaining the product and so on. There may also be some brief exchanges about matters unconnected to the transaction, the weather, how the store seems deserted after the Christmas rush, and so on. The encounter is, for a while at least, memorable and the person who serves me emerges, if only briefly, out of the more general category of shop assistants. There may be small differences between strangers and fleeting acquaintances but these small differences make the difference.

In fact, as I have argued, fleeting encounters are of two kinds. One kind, exemplified by the members' table in London clubs or dinner parties, is closest to what Simmel defines as 'pure sociability'. Here, the importance is in terms of the sociability itself; it is not a means to some other end. In formal terms business (or symbols of business such as the briefcase or the mobile phone) may be banned. Of course, remembering the number of political or economic deals that may at least opened up on such occasions, the lack of instrumentality may exist more on the surface than in reality. Nevertheless, the overt purpose of such events might be defined in terms of pure sociability and there may indeed be formal or informal rules inhibiting the discussion of business or 'shop talk' on such occasions. Further, the structuring of the event in advance through, for example, seating plans, might underline the sociable nature of the occasion. Thus, members of obvious couples might be separated and some kind of gender balance might be attempted. Simmel's brief reference to the 'quartorzieme' ([1903]1971) – the person who makes himself available to complete a dinner party that might otherwise consist of thirteen members – is instructive here. The assumption here would seem to be that a relative stranger with some social skills could be deployed to maintain the sociability at the dinner table.

This idea of pure sociability is reinforced by the likelihood that the hosts at one dinner party are likely to be guests at some other future gathering. This is not necessarily a matter of exact reciprocity but probably a more generalized or serialized reciprocity indicating that both hosts and guests are bound by the same rules of sociability.

Of course, the acquaintances generated through these social events may become more than fleeting acquaintances. They may be passing acquaintances or friends. But, again, many of them will not and the conversation, however animated and stimulating, may turn out to be a one-off affair. This should not necessarily be a matter for regret; it is in the nature of fleeting acquaintances.

Taking a wider perspective we may ask whether sociability is ever really 'pure' and that even where the transaction of business is barred or does not take place, some wider covert instrumentality is at work. What may appear as pure sociability from the point of view of the participants might seem like the maintenance of class and status group solidarities from a more external standpoint. If we view class and status groups as sets of practices rather than as fixed elements in social structure, the pureness of the sociability becomes somewhat modified. Thus it can be argued that even fleeting or passing acquaintances may be significant in terms of maintaining social divisions and locating individuals within hierarchies of power and status.

Much, however, depends on the standpoint and the distance of the observer from the observed. At a suitable analytical distance, such functionalities related to class and status might seem entirely appropriate. Closer up, within the actual day-to-day practices, things may look different and apparent solidarities may dissolve into numerous other distinctions and subdistinctions. By using the phrase 'class and status groups' I intend to convey the multiplicity of divisions that might be found around a single dinner table or at a similar social gathering. There will be differences in life experiences as well as in life chances and the exchange of these experiences might be part of the successful operation of pure sociability. Whether bored or excited, the individual may be provided with fleeting glances into micro-social worlds other than their own and become aware of ties cutting across the particular groups of which he or she are members. The after-effect of pure sociability might not be quite so profound as those attributed to the participation in a corroboree as analysed by Durkheim, but perhaps the comparison is not all that fanciful.

The other kind of fleeting acquaintance discussed in this chapter is the kind encountered in conducting everyday, or sometimes less everyday, business in urban environments. Here we find the examples of taxi drivers, shop assistants, bartenders and the like. In these examples, instrumentalities – travelling across the city, getting served, buying goods – are obvious and primary. Yet, as we have seen, very few of these encounters are purely instrumental, unlike the exchanges in elementary language training texts or phrase books.

Some kind of exchange over and above what is strictly necessary for the transaction while not inevitable will seem highly likely. The reasons for these apparently redundant additions are numerous. They may be part of the sales technique perfected by the assistant. They may be a means of relieving what might be otherwise a boring or routine encounter. Or there might be a covert ethic of not simply treating the other as a means to an end of sharing, if only fleetingly, a common humanity. Frequently, it may be suggested, all of these elements, and others, are involved in different mixes. As Hochschild (1983) and others have argued, simply because the provider of a service is putting on a performance to ensure a smooth present transaction, and the possibility of future transactions, does not necessarily mean that this provider is not involved in the presentation and does not gain some pleasure in pulling it off well. And, it may be assumed, this pleasure may be enhanced if the consumer or client is a willing co-participant in these exchanges.

Between the purely sociable and the purely instrumental there are, of course, many encounters which involve both. Meetings between colleagues at a conference may be a good example where these two tendencies are closely intertwined. In the course of a week an individual, especially one in an urban context, will have engaged in numerous fleeting encounters. Not all of these will be pleasurable or memorable much beyond the actual time of the encounter. Many of them will involve participating in a mixture of business and social interaction, which Shorthose, writing of the Lace Market area of Nottingham, calls the 'convivial ecology' (Shorthose 2004). But all of them involve, in some small measure, some intimations of human connectedness and of what it means to be an individual and a member of a wider set of social processes. They are part of what Jacobs refers to when she writes of the 'exuberant diversity' (Jacobs [1961]1969: 150) of urban life.

Conclusion

The acquaintances described in this chapter might seem to be on the very fringes of this analysis, perhaps even beyond. Fleeting acquaintances in time and space seem to have much in common with strangers, especially the kinds routinely encountered in urban contexts. But if several of the encounters described here seem to have affinities with encounters with strangers, we are talking about strangers who, perhaps only fleetingly, become something more. This 'something more' is in terms of the degree of knowledge (not always exactly reciprocated) that one party has of the other so that the other becomes something more than simply a short list of categorical features. Just as acquaintances may sometimes become intimates so, too, strangers may slip into the class of acquaintances for a short period of time and in a limited space.

Many of the acquaintances presented in this chapter are employees in various service occupations and hence (as we saw in the chapter on professionals and clients) there is a built-in lack of reciprocity for most of these encounters. Yet for both clients and service workers these encounters may be significant albeit in slightly different ways. For the employee the various kinds of encounters with clients, pleasant or unpleasant, may form much of the raw material for gossip with co-workers and for the construction of some kind of occupational identity. For the clients, these pleasant or unpleasant encounters may also enter into the kinds of stories that are told to other acquaintances or intimates, and hence also play a part in the construction of personal identities. Even where these subsequent retellings do not take place, the various exchanges, over and above the purely instrumental requirements of the occasion, may become part of the internal conversations that individuals have with themselves. Fleeting acquaintances are important in that, if only for a short while, they are memorable. They may even make one's day.

7 Distant *and* unwanted encounters

Introduction

This chapter may appear to be something of a ragbag. It consists of encounters with con artists, rapists, stalkers, celebrities and fictional characters. It also includes acquaintances that develop or are sustained over the Internet. What, if anything, do these disparate others have in common?

To some extent it should be admitted that many of these acquaintances were found to be remaining after the previous chapters had been completed. It should be clear by now that they all involve some use and accumulation of knowledge of the other and that while they are not intimates, at least in the full sense of the word, they are not strangers either. The term 'acquaintance' would seem to be appropriate in terms of the arguments so far.

However, they are also examples of overlapping themes which, while they have been raised from time to time in the preceding chapters, have not yet been treated and which deserve some fuller examination. These themes do not apply equally to all the examples explored here; nevertheless they seem to provide some loose affinities which seem to be worth developing further.

The first theme involves a recognition that not all acquaintances may be welcomed. In seeking to present the argument that acquaintances should be taken seriously and seen as something other than belonging to a residual category, I may have over-stressed the more positive side of these relationships. References to the strength of weak ties, ontological security, social capital and so on will certainly reinforce this impression. But, if we think of bullies in the playground or at the workplace, the experiences of being stalked, harassed or assaulted, or others whom we simply find boring or vaguely disagreeable, we can begin to modify this apparently uniformly positive construction. These are all examples of acquaintanceship but they are, to varying degrees, involving unwanted or unpleasant knowledge.

The second is to do with questions of reciprocity. Clearly, there is a certain lack of reciprocity in the examples considered in the previous paragraph in that the other seeks to impose himself or herself on to an unwilling recipient. However, there is some reciprocity in that the recipient responds to the other in certain ways and that these responses (as in the case of stalking) may be incorporated by the other. There are other modes of non-reciprocity, however. Extreme cases might be those to do with relationships between a fan and a celebrity or between a reader and a fictional character. The knowledge which the former has of the latter will greatly outweigh any knowledge that the latter has of the former, which could well be zero in many cases.

A third question is to do with embodiment. We have already encountered this in a previous chapter in considering certain modern working environments such as call centres or helplines. Helpline workers, for example, do have their regular callers and these take on the character of acquaintances. However, the nature of the interaction is disembodied. This contrasts with most of the various other acquaintanceship outlined in this book; neighbours, workmates, professionals and passing and fleeting acquaintances are all embodied, in that they are seen to inhabit particular and recognizable bodies. Indeed, part of the knowledge that acquaintances have of each other is of their bodily appearance; this is part of what makes a particular acquaintance non-substitutable.

Increasingly, however, numerous disembodied encounters are sought after and enjoyed through the Internet. Some sense of bodily appearance may enter into these encounters as when photographs or video material may be used. However, these others may be simply a name, sometimes a name which is used simply for the purposes of relationships in cyberspace. In some cases, gender, age and other marks of identity might be disguised.

These are three themes that seem to be worthy of further development in this chapter: the nature of 'negative' acquaintances; the importance of a lack of reciprocity; and the role of disembodiment. These cover most of the examples considered in this chapter and often overlap with each other in specific cases.

False friends and unwanted acquaintances

Stalkers

'Stalking' and 'stalkers' are words that have appeared more frequently in the media and everyday speech in recent years although this is not to say that the practice itself is new. Celebrity culture may have contributed to this entry of stalking into public discourse but the actual experience of being stalked is much more widespread. In a survey conducted from Leicester University in 2004, it was estimated that one in five women and one in twenty men will be the victims of stalkers at some time in their life (Bindel 2005). A survey conducted by the US National Institute of Justice in 1998 found that 8 per cent of women and 2 per cent of men had been stalked at some stage in their life (Kamir 2001: 205–7). The British Crime Survey of 2004 found that 8 per cent of women and 6 per cent of men interviewed stated that they had been victims of stalking.

Clearly much depends upon the definition of stalking and here, as might be expected, there is considerable fluidity (Finch 2001). Kamir's definition combines the repeated character of the offence with its existential consequences: 'Stalking consists of recurring events that undermine the other

Distant *and* unwanted encounters 93

person's control over his or her own time and space' (Kamir 2001: 15). The British Crime Survey in 1998 distinguished between various degrees of seriousness: 'any persistent and unwanted attention', 'resulting in alarm or distress' and 'resulting in fear of violence' (Finch 2001: 5). However defined, and hence however prevalent, stalking is clearly an unpleasant experience for those on the receiving end. But how does it relate to our discussion of acquaintanceship?

In the case of the women in the 2004 British Crime Survey cited above, 37 per cent of the stalking incidents were perpetrated by former intimates. However, and more important for our present purposes, 59 per cent were perpetrated by other known persons (with 7 per cent by strangers). As we have seen, the boundaries are often fluid but it can be assumed that many of these will be what we have described as acquaintances. Indeed, Finch points out that the distinction between intimate (or, in this case, 'sexual partner'), acquaintance and stranger has been used in the analysis of stalking (2001: 53). Later she stresses the importance of acquaintances: 'a good deal of stalking involves acquaintances, especially where one party fosters a non-reciprocal desire to develop a closer relationship' (p. 153).

The workplace is an important source of this acquaintance-based stalking where it is often closely akin to sexual harassment. In 40 case studies outlined by Finch (2001), six were work based and 15 were based on locality or some other dimension of acquaintanceship. In one case a woman was followed for over 3 years by a man who lived in the flat opposite. He also made approaches to her at work and in friends' houses. In another case, the stalker was a young man who worked at a local garden centre. These cases, briefly outlined in Finch's study, serve us as a reminder of the everyday character of stalking as something far removed from the more frequently reported celebrity cases.

This form of acquaintanceship is clearly unwelcome to the recipients. Physical and mental violence is frequently involved and the recipients may have to go to extreme lengths in order to try to free themselves from the unwanted attention, including moving house (on several occasions in some cases), changing job and calling in the police. We have here a clear example of a form of acquaintanceship that creates a sense of insecurity and which, indeed, can be said to call into question many taken for granted features of everyday life. These will include daily routines and everyday activities such as picking up the telephone when it rings. As Kamir notes, it is 'an assault on a person's self-perception' (2001: 17).

Yet we are clearly dealing with a form of acquaintanceship. Both parties have a degree of knowledge of the other although, in this case, there is a lack of reciprocity in the ways in which the knowledge might be acquired, the kinds of knowledge possessed and the overall meanings attributed to it. The recipient has some prior knowledge of the perpetrator, intimate in some cases and more of a regular acquaintanceship in others. The experience of being stalked forces a reappraisal of this knowledge and places it in a different frame of reference. The stalker, again, also has prior knowledge but will go to considerable lengths to gain further detailed knowledge of the everyday life of the victim.

There is, therefore, a lack of reciprocity in terms of overall perspectives between the two parties although the relationship as a whole has a kind of unwanted reciprocity in that it is definitely a relationship. Thus, victims are advised never to respond to any of the proposals or suggestions that may be made over the telephone. The mere fact of being required *not* to respond is at the same time a recognition of the other and of his claims, however unwelcome, upon you. Fictional accounts (Highsmith 1999; McEwan 1997) have been particularly effective in showing how even the most negative moves on the part of the recipient might be taken as indications of their real interest in the stalker.

More general considerations

I could have included several other examples of unwelcome acquaintances in this section: bullies at school or work, various kinds of interpersonal assaults and harassment, gossip columnists, and so on. The point is not to provide a comprehensive overview of the field but rather to begin to explore some more general principles.

In order to do this I make a somewhat simplistic distinction between victim and perpetrator, realizing that not all the examples fall clearly into these categories. However, it assists in developing more general points. In the first place, the victim clearly has knowledge of the perpetrator, although the range of this knowledge may be considerable. An assault, unwelcome attention, an attempt to swindle may all be short lived if unpleasant but they all provide the victim with knowledge of the other which, in most cases, goes beyond the mere categorical. For example, and I am sure that my experiences are not unique here, when I lived in Manchester I was frequently approached on more than one occasion by the same beggar with exactly the same story. This man needed money to get to a hostel, this man need to go for a job interview, and so on. Similarly, on three separate occasions, an Italian sounding gentlemen tried to sell me a suit at a much reduced rate, explaining that he was returning to Manchester airport that very minute. Although I was one of any number of potential marks for these others, I developed a small amount of knowledge about them which went beyond the categorical. I might, for example, be able to identify them from photographs.

This knowledge that the victim has of the perpetrator is likely to be the greater if both are within relatively closed or bounded locations such as schools, prisons, places of work and some residential communities. Here the knowledge may be the result of direct observation or early encounters or it may be through gossip and local understandings. It is likely that Flashman, the bully in Thomas Hughes's *Tom Brown's Schooldays*, was known to Tom Brown well in advance of any actual encounter and that this knowledge went beyond knowing that he was a bully. A more complex process of acquaintanceship takes place in Patrick Hamilton's brilliant fictional study of micro-tyranny, *The Slaves of Solitude*. The central character, Miss Roach, gradually comes to know her fellow boarders at the Rosamund Tea Rooms during the Second World War. This includes Mr Thwaites who had seemed 'very nice' at first. However, as acquaintanceship developed: 'But now, after more than a year of it, Mr. Thwaites was president in hell' (Hamilton 2006, [1947]: 10). Over the years, Miss Roach came to recognize and dread the verbal ways in which Mr Thwaites asserted his dominance at meal times, especially in relation to vulnerable women. This small, closed environment, made even more so by the bombing raids and the blackout, is a particularly appropriate setting for the exercise of this form of gendered power.

In the second place, the perpetrator frequently deliberately seeks to gain knowledge of the victim and to deploy this knowledge against the victim. This is clearly the case with stalking where often quite detailed knowledge of the everyday practices of the victim is gained and subsequently used in conducted further unwelcome intrusions. Something similar is true, although in different ways, of various types of swindles or confidence tricks, especially in the case of something like identity theft. This contrasts with more everyday forms of acquaintanceship where the knowledge gained is accumulated in a piecemeal and haphazard manner, sometimes over a long period of time.

A rather complex example of the way in which such knowledge is gained and used is provided by a magazine article on women gossip columnists (Vernon 2006). One of these, Katie Nicholl, is described as:

> professionally obligated to insinuate herself (illicitly or otherwise) into fashionable parties, glamorous book launches, and high-profile charitable events in the name of acquiring gossip – gossip which she then shares with her 5 million readers via the medium of her weekly columns
> (p. 26)

Acquaintanceship, and the knowledge associated with it, is relevant here in a variety of ways. Acquaintances are developed and used in order to gain access to appropriate events and sites. These events themselves are frequently characterized by the elaboration of acquaintances and networks of weak ties. Using these contacts and participation in these events is in order to gain knowledge of particular celebrities which can then be used in writing gossip columns. This more deliberate gaining of knowledge and development of acquaintanceship may merge with the more everyday acquaintanceship knowledge. Another gossip columnist is quoted as saying: 'But you never switch off, that's the thing. And everybody's a source. Friends, family . . . it can get embarrassing actually' (Vernon 2006: 28).

In most cases, therefore, the 'perpetrator' deliberately seeks to gain knowledge of the 'victim' and to make use of this knowledge to their advantage. A possible reversal of this is in the case of some forms of acquaintance rape where the person accused of rape is a prominent sportsman (Benedict 1997, 1998). In some cases the woman has, as a fan, acquired a great deal of knowledge of the perpetrator prior to the sexual assault. The victim, on the other hand, is more likely to be seen by the perpetrator as one of a series of sources of sexual gratification.

More generally, these more unwelcome forms of acquaintanceship are characterized by, often, a considerable lack of reciprocity. This is partly a question of different definitions of the situation, based on different degrees and kinds of knowledge. We found something similar in the case of professional-client relationships. In the case of some stalking relationships this lack of reciprocity is both in terms of definition of the situation and the amount and kind of knowledge that one has of the other. In the case of the gossip columnist, it is more likely that columnist and subject will share overlapping social worlds (gossip columnists often become celebrities in their own right) although there may still be marked differences in terms of goals and definition of the situation.

Issues of reciprocity

This brings us more centrally into discussions of reciprocity. Within the whole spectrum of interpersonal relationships there are different expectations of reciprocity. In some cases, reciprocity may be a reasonable expectation on the part of both parties and, indeed, possibly, an obligation. This is seen most clearly in the case of some intimate relationships such as friends or lovers where part of the definition of the relationship involves some notion of mutual disclosure (Jamieson, 1998). There is often a divergence between the expectations and the reality; nevertheless, it may be part of the shared definition of the situation and apparent departures from these expectations might be seen as legitimate causes for complaint.

However, some degree of reciprocity in terms of the offering and receiving of knowledge might have a much wider relevance. In order to take part in the conversations and gossip that are part of relationships between neighbours and colleagues some degree of reciprocity may be expected. Thus if a neighbour volunteers her occupation, you may be expected to provide similar information. It is doubtful whether strict equivalence is required but a clear imbalance in terms of the knowledge exchanged might lead to accusations of snobbery or standoffishness.

There is also the question of reciprocity in principle. In other words, there may be little actual sharing between people who might be defined as acquaintances but it always remains a possibility. Further, the simple fact of seeing or meeting another person on a regular basis may, as we have seen, allow for the 'exchange' of information even if no words are spoken. The possibilities of more overt sharing remain.

There is one form of acquaintanceship where reciprocity is minimal, perhaps even non-existent. This is the relationship that a fan has with a celebrity, say a music performer, a sports star or a television personality. The most the fan can usually expect to get in return is an autograph or a signed photograph. On the fan's side we have, in contrast, an accumulation of knowledge about the celebrity's achievements and everyday, supposedly 'private', life. The accumulation of such knowledge is now greatly enhanced by magazines such as *Hello* and websites on the Internet. The celebrity is aware of fans in general but has little, if any, detailed knowledge of individual fans.

Relations with celebrities are clearly much part of a world in which increasingly global means of communication play an ever more important role. The development of newspapers and large circulation magazines and books in the nineteenth century provided the roots of the modern celebrity/ fan acquaintanceship. The nineteenth century also saw, according to Sennett, the rise of the spectator: 'Passive in public yet still believing in public life'

(Sennett 1974: 195). We may want to argue about the word 'passive'; we only have to recall the crowds that gathered after the death of the Princess of Wales or who watched the funeral of the Queen Mother to reflect on the inappropriateness of this term. What is important about Sennett's comment is that it reminds us that spectatorship, even in its more modern forms, involves some kind of insertion into public life, a realm outside immediate circles of friends and family. Rojek's distinction between notoriety and renown is relevant here. The latter 'follows from personal contact with the individual' located within social networks. This relates more clearly to most of the forms of acquaintanceship discussed in previous chapters. The former applies more to the relationship between a fan and a celebrity (Rojek 2001: 12).

Before continuing this discussion it is worth reminding ourselves that 'celebrities' do not form a unified collection of others. There are differences between the responses of fans to movie stars and responses to other celebrities such as TV personalities and pop stars and so on (Marshall 1997). Relations between fans and movie stars have the longer history and have probably received the greatest critical attention. However, each set of relationships has its own special features. It is argued, for example, that the development of the close-up was a major factor in the development of the Hollywood star system. This provides for an intimate (and non-reciprocal) knowledge of the other's face, a major element of any knowledge of the other.

If the word 'passive' is relevant it refers less to the activities or orientations of fans themselves but more to the relationship between fan and celebrity and to the clear lack of reciprocity. The relationship, in Rojek's words: 'frequently involve unusually high levels of non-reciprocal emotional dependence' (p. 51). Rojek uses the term 'para-social' to describe this relationship, a term also used by Gans in writing about relationships between members of the community he was studying and performers like Frank Sinatra (Gans 1965: 191). Again, the use of the term 'para-social' tells us something about the relationship itself and the marked lack of reciprocity. The performer is aware of and, to some extent, depends upon fans in general; the fan has detailed knowledge of and interest in the performer as an individual.

The reference to Gans's study also reminds us of the importance of relationships between fans. The relationship between fan and celebrity is frequently mediated through more significant others. In the example provided by Gans, the life and career of Sinatra clearly had a resonance for Americans of Italian origin. Other examples where identification with a performer or a celebrity has a strong communal base are numerous; a few random examples might include footballers Stanley Matthews ('The Potteries') and George Best (Northern Ireland) and the *Coronation Street* star, Pat Phoenix (Manchester). One well-documented example is that of the construction of stars such as Judy Garland as gay icons (Dyer 2004). Even without this more obvious communal support, the relationship with celebrities may be mediated through fan clubs, websites or more informal social networks.

It is said that one of the most frequently asked questions about Queen Elizabeth II is 'what is she really like?' and this question probably applies to many other public figures as well (Littler 2004). The kind of knowledge that a fan or supporter gains or seeks about a public figure is not based upon the public persona alone. In part, this may reflect a desire – the 'emotional dependence' that Rojek refers to – to establish a more personal relationship with the celebrity, to have access to some privileged information that is available to a select few. It may reflect a particular notion of an 'inner truth' about an individual, an awareness of the backstage of a performer's life. In a sense we are all Goffmans now. In the absence of direct contact, such approximations of what a celebrity is really like emerge through casual conversations and 'friends of friends' as well as through the increasingly important activities of gossip columnists. It is likely that this leads to a constantly shifting boundary between the public and the private. Once certain aspects of a 'private' life become public, further aspects of a 'real self' await discovery.

There are three further points to be made about these relationships with celebrities. The first is that the death of a celebrity does not end the relationship. One only has to think of performers such as Edith Piaf, Marilyn Monroe and Elvis Presley to realize that the accumulation of knowledge on the part of fans and followers continues long after death and that an important part of that question was to discover what they were 'really like' as well as to establish links between their public work, their songs or films, and their private lives.

A second point is to remind ourselves that this fan/celebrity relationship is not confined to adolescents or the readers of magazines such as *Hello*. A great deal of modern political debate, for example, is conducted around individual personalities and leaders. Again, the desire is to understand what the President or the Prime Minister is really like and what really went on behind the scenes. The BBC television interviewer, Jeremy Paxman, just before the Iraq war, asked Prime Minister Tony Blair whether he and George W Bush 'prayed together' at their last meeting. The belief was, clearly, that this private activity might have some importance for public decisions. Outside the world of national and international politics, lower participants in large organizations may speculate about the real character of their CEOs. And such discussion about the 'real' character of significant figures in the profession, is not unknown among sociologists.

Finally, there are links here with the previous section where I discussed the stalking relationship. There are clear affinities here: the lack of reciprocity and the accumulation of knowledge about the other, for example. The activity of a fan may sometimes be seen as a form of stalking and the boundaries may become quite blurred. At what point does the dedicated autograph hunter become a stalker?

What this brief analysis of relationships with celebrities tells us is that, despite some important differences, these relationships can round out our understanding of acquaintanceship. It reminds us of the mediated and fragmented character of the knowledge that exists between acquaintances:

> The various mediated constructions of the film celebrity ensures [sic] that whatever intimacy is permitted between the audience and the star is purely at the discursive level . . . Depending on the level of commitment of the audience member, certain types of fragments or traces of identity are deemed adequate.
>
> (Marshall 1997: 90)

What is distinct about this form of acquaintanceship, however, is its intertextuality (p. 58). Knowledge of a movie star or pop singer is mediated through the films and songs, the numerous writings in fan magazines and the people to whom the celebrities are linked. However, this knowledge constitutes a form of cultural capital (Fiske 1992). It has a value in the context of peer groups (i.e. other sets of acquaintances) and can be important in the process of constructing an identity and linking the public with the private. At the very least, consideration of the fan/celebrity relationship in terms of acquaintanceship can provide a counterbalance to more pathological models of fandom (Lewis 1992).

Close to acquaintanceship with celebrities are relations with fictional characters. In some cases (John Wayne, Sylvester Stallone, Marilyn Monroe) there is a merging with a living actor and a fictional character or a series of similar fictional characters. The large following that programmes like *Star Trek* develop is in part due to the fusion of characters with the actors who play them (Jenkins 1992). However, here I am concerned with the way in which individuals develop acquaintanceship with characters in novels or fictional representations (such as soap operas), which are less dependent upon the players who represent them.

It is likely that the serialized production of much fiction in the nineteenth century contributed to the development of fictional characters as acquaintances, and sometimes even intimates. The gradual accumulation of knowledge about a character over time and with periodic gaps of a week or more in some ways mimics the acquaintanceship process, which is also built up over time. Unlike relationships with celebrities, there are no gossip columnists to tell us what Mr Pickwick, Sherlock Holmes or Harry Potter are 'really' like. Paradoxically, therefore, the acquaintanceship with a fictional character, because it is less mediated, may be more authentic than a relationship with a celebrity. Readers identified with Mr Pickwick and other members of his club and shared in the death of Little Nell. In fact, in these cases, there was some mediation through the author himself, as Dickens went around the country giving popular readings from his works (Ackroyd 1990).

Perhaps one of the best known examples of acquaintance with a fictional character is that of Sherlock Holmes. It is well known that Conan Doyle's attempts to kill off his detective were resisted by his reading public. People wrote to Sherlock Holmes at his fictional address of 221B Baker St and during the 1951 Festival of Britain there was a recreation of the detective's study in the place where this address might have been. Over time, the image of Sherlock Holmes has been created and recreated several times and subsequent representations (pipe, deerstalker cap) have overlaid the original creation while other facts (such as Holmes's drug taking) have been suppressed.

At this point an autobiographical example might be appropriate. During my late childhood (roughly aged 9–12) I developed some kind of identification with a radio character, Dick Barton. Dick Barton was a special agent who featured in a long running serial story on BBC radio. The plots were fairly standard; Barton and his assistants defeated a series of international villains after placing their own lives in danger on numerous occasions. My knowledge of this character was built up, day by day and week by week, through listening to these fifteen minute broadcasts. Occasionally I read pieces in publications such as the *Radio Times*, which rounded out the 'biography' of Barton or provided accounts of the actors who played the central character. However, the core exchange was between myself and the unfolding narratives.

However, there was some mediation in that discussion of Dick Barton frequently took place between myself and my friends. If there were a gender theme in my following of the Dick Barton narratives it was less a matter of identifying with a male hero and more a question of developing an ironic stance to these selfsame narratives. We derived pleasure from unmasking and parodying the narrative conventions and so, it seems in retrospect, deriving a measure of control over the characters. We saw ourselves as willing collaborators in the production of a fictional character.

I doubt whether these experiences – of simultaneously enjoying and deconstructing a narrative – were atypical. Certainly an ironic mode is one mode of relating to both celebrities and fictional characters. The point I wish to make is that the relationship with a fictional character, based upon a narrative that unfolds over time, is a form of acquaintanceship in that it involves the accumulation of knowledge of the other although, in this case, unreciprocated. What is suggested here is some kind of relationship between the acquaintanceship process and narratives. I shall return to this theme in the final chapter.

I suggested that even my relationship with Dick Barton was mediated, and probably modified, through interaction with others who followed the same adventures. Jenkins in his detailed study of such relationships around television fictions highlights how important such mediations can be. Followers of *Star Trek*, for example, reject the derogatory term 'Trekkie', preferring 'Trekkers' instead (Jenkins 1992: 21). This shows the complexity of these mediations for not only has the programme itself become the subject of media comment and scholarly analysis, knowledge and opinion, which is also filtered through the groups of fans, but the fans themselves have become incorporated into the media discussions. Jenkins shows how the followers of particular programmes are far from passive consumers but constitute overlapping communities over the Internet and actively engage in seeking to shape the programmes or to respond creatively (writings new scripts or poems) to the narratives and characters.

As an example, consider some of the judgements that fans made about an American TV programme, *Beauty and the Beast*:

'Vincent can be sensitive without being wimpy'
'Catherine is my favourite character on the show . . . I find Catherine to be tough, resourceful, reliable. She can take care of herself. But she's also allowed to cry'.

(Jenkins 1992: 140–1)

Again we see how the acquaintanceship process works, certainly in relation to fictional characters but perhaps more generally as well. This knowledge is built up through both following the narratives themselves but also through exchanging ideas and opinions with others. Further, this is not simply factual knowledge of the other's biography. It also involves some kind of moral evaluation of the other and through this some construction of the self and of more general notions of gendered identities.

Disembodied acquaintances?

Up to now the acquaintances with which we have been concerned have the shared characteristic of embodiment. We can say that part of the knowledge that we have of acquaintances of any kind is their embodied character: their physical appearance, their movement, their directly observable modes of being in the world. (Where there is some visual impairment, other senses may serve as indicators of the embodied character of acquaintances.) Conversely, of course, our embodied characteristics make us available as acquaintances to others.

Perhaps a main point of embodied recognition is the other person's face. Everyday conversational practices seem to require that we not only listen to the other but also observe the other's face in order, for example, to scan for signs of irony or a flash of annoyance in conveying what might otherwise be straightforward information or comment. People routinely say 'I remember the face' while confessing that they have forgotten a name. This reference to the face is frequently a shorthand term for a whole collection of embodied characteristics, including tone of voice, physical presence and context. However, the face remains an important element in the identification of an acquaintance.

All this remains true, not only for neighbours and colleagues at work, those whom we meet on a regular basis, but also for more casual or fleeting acquaintances. Indeed, it can be argued that the less detailed our knowledge of an acquaintance, the more important are these embodied characteristics. Even where we have little or no knowledge of the other's biography our apprehension of the other as an embodied acquaintance provides for this degree of non-substitutability that distinguishes an acquaintance from a stranger.

Embodiment remains important even where, as in the cases dealt with in the last section, there is a lack of reciprocity. Sports personalities, television performers, film stars and all other celebrities are available as embodied others. Indeed, not only is this embodied knowledge all that a fan can reliably possess (since access to the 'real' other is highly mediated), embodiment and embodied performance is frequently what defines the celebrity in the first place. The same is true for fictional characters: Mr Pickwick, Sherlock Holmes and Harry Potter are clearly embodied individuals. But for both celebrities and fictional characters, the fan, for the most part, remains disembodied except as part of a mass of fans.

However, there are increasing signs that other forms of acquaintanceship can have a disembodied character. This is not an entirely new phenomenon. Radio stars and fictional characters in radio shows were of course popular long before the dominance of television. It can be argued that this is a form of embodiment, partly because the personalities were the subject of newspaper comments and publicity photographs and partly because the voice, and apprehension of the voice, is a form of embodied access. What Roland Barthes described as 'the grain of the voice' (Barthes 1972) refers to a characteristic that is embodied in both origin and in terms of the imaginative engagement of the listener.

We have also already discussed the kind of disembodied access that is available through call centres and helplines. Again, the voice is central to this mode of acquaintanceship. However, our concern here is with the development of email and the Internet and the possibilities that these raise for the growth of a form of acquaintanceship that is relatively disembodied but often also reciprocal. I say relatively because Internet communication can include the use of photographs or physical descriptions.

The extent and nature of the significance of these developments has been much debated but we are certainly dealing with matters of considerable complexity. Towards the end of 2007, readers of some British newspapers read about Emma Clarke who had been providing announcements on the London underground system. These announcements themselves are examples of disembodied communications, albeit of a rather limited kind. However, she gained some notoriety (and lost her job) after putting some spoof announcements on to her website. One example went: 'We would like to remind our American tourist friends that you are almost certainly talking too loudly.' This became another form of disembodied communication in which she emerged as an acquaintance for all those who visited her website. She lost her job after it appeared that some of these announcements seemed to be criticizing the underground service. The publicity attached to this case provides another twist to the story (Topping 2007).

To begin with email. The overwhelming number of people that I communicate directly with using email are already known to me and the email communication is part of an ongoing acquaintanceship that is also maintained by other means. Thus although the form of communication is disembodied the relationship as a whole is not. There are some people that I 'met' first on the Internet (editors, conference organizers) and there are just a few who are solely known to me via this means.

However, the balance between email-only acquaintances and others where email communication is part of a wider set of practices presumably varies between individuals. Some of the debate around 'netiquette' is concerned more with email communication between people who might otherwise be strangers or unknown to each other. Here, again, we find the familiar desires to find a balance between intimacy and distance. How far is it appropriate to sign off a first communication with you with a first name only and a couple of kisses? (Jeffries 2007) How do you respond when a first communication begins with 'Hi, David!'? Does the use of emoticons, highly stylized representations, simply represent a shifting of the boundaries between intimacy and distance in the context of email communication? What does appear to be clear is that a new form of communication raises novel concerns but also reflect deeper dilemmas in the relationships between acquaintances.

Another area which I shall touch on briefly is that of virtual assistants on the Internet, sometimes known as 'chat bots', short for 'chat robot' (Gustavsson 2005; Turkle 1996). Here we have commercial and non-commercial organizations deploying virtual assistants on their websites, in order to provide appropriate information. Some of these may clearly be cartoon characters but of particular interest to us are those that take on human form, some of which being animated photos and the others 'photo-unreal', 'realistic compositions that have been made to look human' (Gustavsson 2005: 408). These representations are strongly gendered.

In one sense, these virtual assistants transcend the embodied/disembodied distinction. The information or advice that they provide could be delivered through other, more conventional, means. However, they are represented in human form and are provided with limited biographies and are able to have conversations with clients. But their answers may remind the questioner of their non-human origins. In answer to the interviewer's question, 'do you have a family?', one chat bot replies: 'I am a machine; hence I have no family'. However, another is given a limited biography: 'I've got three children and my wife and I have been happily married for 14 years. That's all I want to say about my private life' (Gustavsson 2005: 411).

In terms of our discussion so far, these virtual assistants may become forms of acquaintances in that they are distinguishable from other chat bots and have limited biographies which are accessible to the visitor to the website. There is some kind of reciprocity taking place although the range of answers that the VAs are able to provide are, again, limited and ultimately constrained by the goals of the organization concerned. The extent to which these exchanges might go is illustrated in the title of Shelley Turkle's chapter, 'Making a pass at a robot' (Turkle 1996). They have some affinities with some fleeting acquaintances (shop assistants, for example) as well as with fictional characters. They certainly deserve a place in our discussion of acquaintanceship.

In passing it might be noted that people quite frequently give names to their computers (Turkle 1996). This is not to say, presumably, that people treat their computers as if they were exactly the same as human beings but does indicate a recognition that they belong to a wider sphere of human activity. The very term, 'personal computer' indicates a kind of relationship between a self and a machine, part of what Lury calls 'prosthetic' culture (Lury 1998).

My main concern, however, is with interactions between humans over the Internet in chat rooms, blogs and websites such as 'MySpace' or 'Facebook'. These sites are clearly of considerable importance and increasing numbers of people make use of them for increasing periods of time. Individuals may use these sites to share and develop common interests, for networking or to develop friendships. While some of the relationships established may be described (at least by the participants) as intimates many of them would seem to be closer to acquaintances.

Rather than attempt to cover the whole, and rapidly growing, field, I shall give a couple of illustrations and then attempt to explore some more general issues. My first illustration comes from an article in *Newsweek* (Vencat 2007): 'Like millions of teenagers around the world, Sue Bloom spends several hours socializing online every day. She posts pictures, meets new friends, updates her blog and runs a popular online photography group with almost 500 members.' However, the author of this article goes on to point out that Sue is not a teenager but a '58-year-old art historian'. The article deals with 'Eons.com', where you have to be at least 50 to join. This is key to the argument that these baby boomers or 'silver surfers' could be the future of online networking.

This article, with the reference to posting pictures, highlights the limits of the term 'disembodied' in the title of this section. However, it also demonstrates the importance of the Internet in the lives of people at some distance from the stereotyped teenagers and its increasing role in the elaboration of acquaintances. The article may use the term 'friends' and doubtless this usage is shared by Sue and by many participants. However, it is likely that some of those encountered through this site might also be described as acquaintances and have all the features of acquaintanceship outlined in previous chapters. The article also suggests that Internet usage may reproduce some of the social divisions present in the wider society, in this case generation.

A second case is rather different. In 2006, a 17-year-old girl, Anna Svidersky, was stabbed to death in Vancouver, Washington. After Anna's friends had posted a tribute to the murdered teenager on MySpace, the news of her death went around the world: 'People started taking virtual pilgrimages to Anna's profile while others made visual tributes and posted them online' (Jonze 2006: 14). One of those who received the news, a teenager in Oxfordshire, said that 'you could find out nearly everything about her'. Although only approved MySpace friends could leave comments on Anna's site, an alternative site was set up for those who wish to continue to make tributes. The whole event is likened by some to the responses to the death of Princess Diana, although in this case the tributes are being paid to someone who, prior to her death, had no public profile.

These and other examples raise a variety of interesting problems in the study of acquaintances. In the first place, are we dealing with acquaintances rather than, say, friends where a greater degree of intimacy is presumed? Once the contact has been made and some information distributed we are not dealing with relationships between strangers. However, although the word 'friend' may frequently be used (as in the '50-plus' example above) there can be some doubt as to whether the word can be used more generally. In other words, it seems likely that there is some discrimination made between friends with whom some intimate or privileged knowledge us exchanged, and those who simply share some common interest and exchange information or views over a period of time. While the Internet may expand an individual's range of intimates (at least in terms of some dimensions of intimacy) it also expands the range of acquaintances. How and where the line is drawn, or if it is drawn at all, is a matter for the individual concerned. From the outside, at least, it would seem that there is some difference in degree.

In the second place, are their any differences in kind between acquaintances developed online and those we have described elsewhere? While online acquaintances may later meet each other as embodied beings, this is not necessarily the case. Further, the distances within online communities may produce contrasts with other locally or work-based communities in that they are, in Delanty's words: 'polymorphous, highly personalised and often expressive' (Delanty 2003: 168). There is a greater element of choice, not only in whether to initiate interaction in the first place but also in the kind and character of the interaction that is conducted. There is a greater potentiality for a kind of playfulness that is perhaps less likely to occur between people who meet, bodily, on a regular day-to-day basis. However, as Delanty also points out, virtual communities may also be established around more traditional bonds such as families, locally based communities or groups of colleagues. Use of the Internet might be a valuable addition to (although probably not a substitute for) the kind of networking that is important for managerial or professional bodies.

There does not seem to be any evidence to suggest that online acquaintances (or friends) are a substitute for other forms of acquaintance. Sometimes, online acquaintances can become 'real' embodied others or exploring cyberspace may be a shared activity between people who are already, or who become, so. There are numerous complex links between virtual and personalized acquaintances. A tentative conclusion should be that the development of virtual communities is part of an overall process of expanding acquaintances in modern society.

However, there is, as with acquaintanceship in general, a darker side to all this. There is a certain liminality of cyberspace (Fox 2004: 226). The apparent existence outside conventional notions of time and space (i.e. being here and now) also appears to weaken other kinds of constraints. Thus, others may not always be what they claim to be; names can be disguised along with details such as age, ethnicity, gender and physical appearance in general. This freedom to be someone else or, at the very least, the freedom that arises from being able to control much of the presentation of self, can be very liberating.

The downside is also obvious. Matters of concern include the grooming of young persons for later sexual encounters or cyberbullying. There are accounts of teenagers suffering from online bullying or harassment or highly negative online gossip (Johnson 2006). Some publicity has been given to the development of suicide websites and chat rooms where information about suicide methods and encouragement may be shared. As with other matters, it is sometimes difficult to assess the significance or novelty of these concerns. Nevertheless, the liminal character of the Internet does seem to play a part and highlights that this form of acquaintance may, too, have its downside.

One of the more persuasive accounts of the significance of Internet communication and computers is provided by Sherry Turkle (1996). She writes of 'taking things at interface value', suggesting that individuals are aware of the differences between computer mediated communications and other face-to-face interactions. Thus when individuals consult a programme called 'Depression 2.0', they normally recognize the limitations of such advice that they might receive. However, within this framework of recognition, they see that the advice might be helpful and provide something that might be worked with. Communications on the Internet provide for an expansion of the interactional sphere, rather than a substitute for it. To this extent there is some affinity with the idea of acquaintanceship or, at least, the approach I am arguing for here.

Therefore it does not necessarily matter that the personalities that one interacts with on the Internet might, in reality, be other than they seem. The same possibilities are open to the initiator of the Internet interaction (say the initial visit to a chat room) as they are to the recipients. Turkle talks about

106 Acquaintances

the 'rapid cycling through different identities' (p. 179). Within these virtual communities, virtual characters interact with each other. The 'MUDs' (Multi-User Domains) 'imply difference, multiplicity, heterogeneity and fragmentation' (p. 185). There is an affinity here with the very idea of acquaintanceship seen as a whole. I have written about a variety of acquaintances in a variety of different spheres and with a variety of different meanings. If a whole set of acquaintances constitutes a social network it is, for the most part, a very loose-knit one. Individuals are able to present different aspects of their self in different contexts. While, normally, this does not entail presenting oneself as having a different gender or ethnicity (or any other characteristic) there is a sense, at least, where we can see everyday acquaintances and relationships on the Internet as possessing certain family resemblances.

Turkle also claims that interactions on the Internet can be seen as replacing what Oldenberg called 'great, good places' (Oldenberg 1991; Turkle 1996: 233). They are more like the idealized bar in the television programme, *Cheers* than any actual existing bar or pub might be. Perhaps this is overstating the case. The kinds of sites that Oldenberg described were probably rarely quite as he describes them (they were frequently limited in terms of class, race and gender, for example) and the alleged decline of such places can also be seen as somewhat exaggerated. However, relations in cyberspace can represent an extension of the sites for interaction and the presentation of different aspects of oneself rather than a substitute for existing, more direct or face-to-face, sites. However one looks at it, acquaintanceship seems to be an appropriate term for many Internet-based contacts.

One final question is whether the word 'disembodied' in the subtitle of this section is appropriate. Stone appears to strike a note of caution where she refers to: 'incontrovertibly social spaces in which people still meet face-to-face, but under new definitions of both "meet" and "face"' (Stone 1994: 85). One might also add 'people' to this list of new definitions. Argyle and Shields similarly question whether Internet communication is disembodied (Argyle and Shields 1996). In (unqualified) face-to-face interaction, social actors are routinely aware of the embodiedness of each other and, through this, of their own embodiedness. This kind of interactive double awarenesss is, to say the least, unlikely in Internet communication. However, embodiment of a kind certainly takes place. Argyle and Shields refer to 'generic actions', the way in which parties to Internet discussions also use words such as 'smile', 'frown', 'grin' and 'smirk' to accompany the other written exchanges (pp. 60–1). The use of emoticons is part of these processes of embodying Internet communication. When the word 'smile' appears on the screen we may well respond appropriately. Thus, in Internet communication, individuals may come to develop emotions and the appropriate physical responses. This includes sexual arousal.

In addition we have already noted how 'in-person servers' or virtual assistants take on embodied forms and are given brief biographies. As with other service workers in the modern world, they are expected to have a smart appearance and an agreeable manner. The more one considers the issue, the more it seems that the term disembodied may not be entirely appropriate. Even where participants take on characteristics quite unlike their 'real' embodied selves (changing age or gender, for example) they are taking pains to present themselves as embodied beings.

Conclusion

This chapter has considered those forms of acquaintances that appear, in one way or another, to depart from the model of acquaintanceship that has been developed in previous chapters. We have acquaintances who are unwelcome, while the implication so far has been that such others are broadly to be welcomed. We have examples where there would appear to be a marked lack of reciprocity (acquaintanceship with celebrities or fictional characters) while in most of the examples discussed previously there would appear to be some degree of reciprocity if not equivalence. And we have examples which appear to question the taken-for-granted embodied character of acquaintances.

In the course of exploring these apparent departures from the accounts presented in earlier chapters we also discover overlaps. Fans may sometimes become stalkers (and their activities may have some affinities with stalking even if actual contact is never made) and bullying and sexual harassment may take place over the Internet. Followers of fictional characters may make contact with other devotees through the Internet and may themselves, as a result, become the subject of media attention or public comment. There is little doubt that consideration of these apparently deviant cases and their possible overlaps considerably rounds out our understanding of acquaintances and the acquaintanceship process. However diverse, what remains is the development and deployment of knowledge to the degree that the other is no longer a stranger but, in some ways, closer to being an intimate.

8 Conclusion

Summary

The key points of my argument should be familiar by now and can be listed as a series of bullet points:

- Acquaintances lie somewhere between intimates and strangers.
- Acquaintanceship can be characterized as a particular form of knowledge of the other, distinct from the categorical knowledge that exists between strangers or the complex meshing of biographies that characterizes relationships between intimates.
- The boundaries between strangers, acquaintances and intimates are fuzzy and there can often be movement between them.
- There are differences within the field of acquaintances. These can be defined according to both the amount of knowledge that one has of the other and the frequency of interaction between them.
- There are also differences in terms of the degree of reciprocity between intimates, ranging from high to low or, possibly, absent.
- A theme running through many forms of acquaintanceship is the idea of some kind of balance between closeness and distance.

There is one further theme which requires some attention. Are acquaintances ascribed or achieved? Within the field of intimates we can find both ascribed or achieved relationships; parents and children and kin relationships tend to be closer to the ascribed (or 'given') end of the continuum while friends and lovers are more readily seen as achieved relations. (As always there is considerable cultural variation here.) In the case of acquaintances, matters seem to be a little more complex. Many acquaintances would seem to be by-products that exist as a result of our pursuing other projects to do with residence, employment, running errands, and so on. To this extent they are ascribed. However, a lot of activities, especially those to do with leisure, are seen as attractive not simply because of the overt aims (organizing charities, going to cultural events, joining clubs) but because they also provide an opportunity to meet other people. And while most of us have to earn a living or to live somewhere, notions of 'a friendly place to work' or 'a good neighbourhood' are also important. There seems to be an interesting combination of ascription and achievement, or choice and necessity, when it comes to acquaintances.

At this point it might be helpful to conduct a thought experiment and imagine a situation without acquaintances. It might be possible to imagine limited cases – children brought up in closed religious sects for example – but these are rare. For the most part, it is difficult to construct such a scenario. One reason why this seems to be very difficult is that it appears to be so much at variance with how we constitute modern life. All the classical accounts of the characteristics of modernity would seem to point in the direction of a greater proportion of acquaintances as a necessary consequence of engaging in the mobilities of life as we understand and experience it today. Even taking a relatively conventional life course involving education (school and a little beyond), employment outside the home and establishing a separate residence will also involve the accumulation of dozens of acquaintances. To this extent we can see acquaintanceship as ascribed.

However, as we have seen, this ascription is often mixed with achievement. There is an element of achievement in deciding 'how far to go' with any particular acquaintances and there is also an element of achievement in the fact that, as we have seen, other sources of acquaintances may be actively sought after. 'Getting out and meeting people' is frequently seen as a desirable activity at different stages of the life course.

And this brings us on to another reason why it is difficult to conduct our thought experiment of an acquaintance-free existence. Not only does it appear to be the case that the routine demands of modern living actually make acquaintances a near inevitability, but also a life without acquaintances would seem to be bereft in some deeper way. It is not that acquaintances may sometimes become intimates or even that they may develop some intimate-like characteristics. It is the fact that acquaintances are not and are different from intimates that is important.

This brief discussion indicates some of the themes that will be taken up in this concluding chapter. I want to bring together some of the suggestions made in previous chapters about the importance of acquaintanceship, importance for individuals, for social life in general and for sociological enquiry. I also want to return to the question about the relationship between acquaintanceship and modernity or late modernity. Put simply, is acquaintanceship growing in importance in later modern society? And, if so, in what ways?

Before embarking on this discussion I shall bring together two other sets of themes that have emerged in the course of the earlier analysis. One is to do with the practices of acquaintanceship, in other words how people *do* acquaintanceship. And the other is to do with the sites of acquaintanceship, where it is *done* and whether some sites are more conducive than others. As elsewhere in this study the discussions are intended to open up areas for further investigation.

The practices of acquaintanceship

In this section I consider how people do acquaintanceship. The fact that many of the practices seem to be totally spontaneous and unrehearsed does not mean that they are not worth considering. The same would also be true of many of the naturalistic observations made by someone like Goffman.

Let us turn to one of the simplest examples of acquaintanceship where I regularly see, let us say, a woman taking her dog for a walk at more-or-less the same time every day. Even without speaking or even acknowledging the other, I am accumulating and storing little fragments of knowledge which mark this person out as being in some ways distinct and unique in my circle of others. In practice, of course, things rarely remain at this elementary level. We may exchange greetings or may use these casual meetings as resources when we meet on elsewhere under different circumstances. Or I might augment my knowledge through a kind of triangulation, asking others about this woman who regularly exercises her labrador. Or, and in addition, I may exercise my imagination and make up narratives about this woman's life based upon others I have encountered or other texts that I have read. The point I wish to stress is that even at the most minimal level of acquaintanceship there is some kind of work on my part in accumulating, making sense of and structuring the knowledge about the other.

Beyond these largely internal and minimal practices, probably the most significant practice of acquaintanceship is conversation. Once the conversation moves beyond such (in Britain at least) inevitable topics as the weather (Fox 2004) there is a process of exchanging small fragments of biography. This may not simply be a matter of exchanging information (where you live, work, or come from) but also to do with questions of tone, personality and facial expressions. Such exchanges, verbal and non-verbal, are part of the process of constructing the other as a particular and distinguishable acquaintance as someone who is distinct from others who might be encountered in similar circumstances.

Clearly conversation takes place between intimates as well so it is not a distinctive practice associated with acquaintanceship. But it might be asked whether there is anything qualitatively different about conversation between acquaintances. It might be hypothesized that the conversational practices between acquaintances are closer to those practices associated with pure sociability, possibly mixed with straightforward instrumentalities (conversations between a regular customer and a local shopkeeper, for example). This sociability may itself be of two types. In the first case we have a high proportion of banter, repeated phrases and relatively 'safe' topics; the kind of exchanges recorded in Roy's 'banana time' come to mind here (Roy 1960). Alternatively, we may have conversations where the conversation – the sociability – is an end in itself. Participants are expected to keep it going and to maintain the overall pleasure of the occasion.

Conversation between intimates, on the other hand, while it may have elements of the above, cannot be limited to them. These conversations may deal with 'dangerous' topics about their relationships, may involve more exposure of the self and may permit or require longer periods of silences. The difference between the two sets of conversational practices might be described by introducing the idea of 'ownership'. In the pure sociability model, participants do not necessarily own the topics or views discussed; what matters is the skill with which they are discussed. In the case of conversations between intimates, there is a stronger notion of ownership and the words used and the views expressed are held to be revelatory in terms of the individual selves or the relationship itself. I am clearly dealing with ideal typifications here but these differences can be seen as variations on the theme of closeness and distance, raised at several points in this discussion.

It should be noted that this is not a contrast between the 'deep' conversations between intimates and the 'shallow' chat between acquaintances. As the reference to the idea of sociability indicates, both have their place. Similarly, the conversation between acquaintances might be defined as 'gossip' with all the connotations of idle chit-chat. However, gossip, as has often been maintained (Bergmann 1993; Gluckman 1963) is an important social activity despite the fact (and possibly because of the fact) that it is so often deplored. Again, the practice of gossip is not confined to talk between acquaintances; clearly it also takes place between intimates. However, gossip is an important mode of defining acquaintances.

This can be elaborated by considering what Bergmann (1993) calls the 'gossip triangle': A gossips to B about C. In order that this may take place, there has to be some degree of knowledge about C that is shared between A and B. It is possible that any two or all three of the participants may be intimates. However, they do not need to be intimates; the minimal demand is that they be acquaintances. To participate in gossip or to be the subject of gossip is part of the way in which acquaintances are defined.

One aspect of gossip, and one that is often equally deplored, is 'name dropping'. 'Name dropping' might be defined as a particular kind of claim in relation to past or present acquaintances. It does not apply to intimate relations. 'Lloyd George knew my father' may be name dropping; 'Lloyd George was my father' is a different kind of claim (Hague 2008: viii). Name dropping also requires an assumption of shared knowledge between the conversational partners; 'My father met Barack Obama' works in the way that 'My father met Fred Bloggs' does not. Examples of name dropping outside of routine conversational practices occur with considerable frequency in the autobiographies of public figures and the practice may be seen as part of the process of constructing an autobiographical self.

One final practice, linked to conversational practices, is to do with networking. Again, this can be seen as a process of making use of acquaintances and developing acquaintances; a good example would be the work of the gossip columnists noted in the previous chapter. Networking is a practice closely associated with acquaintances. This example comes from a volume of autobiography by the historian, Arnold J. Toynbee which is called, significantly enough, *Acquaintances* (Toynbee 1967: 215):

> Before setting out for India, Mr Crane [Charles R Crane] needed to meet the author of *A Passage to India*. Did I know Mr E.M. Forster? Could I tell Mr Crane where he lived? Could I give Mr Crane an introduction to him?
>
> I happened to know where Mr Forster lived, because the place was the home-town of the archaeologist F.W. Hasluck, who had been the librarian of the British School at Athens when I had been a student there in 1911–12 . . .

In fact, Toynbee had met Forster only briefly on a couple of occasions and found the task something of an embarrassment. It seems that nothing came of this request. This is a beautiful example of the complexities of networking (combined with a bit of name dropping) and their role in the construction of an autobiographical self.

All these examples of the practices of acquaintanceship (and there are undoubtedly others) are not simply things that people defined as acquaintances do. In engaging in these practices – gossip, name dropping, networking, etc. – individuals are also constituting and reproducing particular acquaintances and the idea, more generally, of acquaintanceship.

Sites of acquaintanceship

I have discussed the practices of acquaintanceship – what acquaintances do. But where does acquaintanceship take place? Are there any particular sites of acquaintanceship?

From what has gone before it might be argued that acquaintanceship can take place anywhere. I have discussed places of work, neighbourhoods and leisure areas. Acquaintanceship can take place in department stores, taxis, consulting rooms or on railway stations. It is perhaps easier to indicate where acquaintanceship is less likely to take place and that is (at least in modern British society) in the area of private space defined as 'home' (see Holdsworth and Morgan 2005: 68–86). Acquaintanceship is strongly associated with public spaces.

However, the term 'public' is a difficult one and there are numerous overlapping and situationally defined meanings of this complex term. Perhaps all that can be said at this point is that acquaintanceship is more likely to take place in places defined as public or which have some public elements in them. Conversely, acquaintanceship is less likely to develop in sites defined wholly or largely as private. But are there any particular sites that are more conducive to acquaintanceship?

There would seem to be three characteristics of such public or semi-public spaces:

1   They are places where it is not only possible for people to congregate but that it is expected that they do so. Thus while there are all kinds of nodal positions in cities where people pass each other, often in large numbers, they are not expected to linger there. Indeed places like railway stations and shopping malls seem to be designed to inhibit such lingering and people who pass through them are expected to be travellers or consumers. These sites contrast with places – like some parks or squares – where gathering and lingering are central to the rationale of the place.
2   As implied above, people are expected not simply to pass through or to be in such spaces but to spend some time there.
3   At the same time there is a fair amount of movement in and out of such spaces.

Some of these places may be clubs and associations, which often have a variety of overt functions but which also seem to exist to encourage sociability.

Even quite small communities may have several such associations which may constitute the foci of everyday social life (Frankenberg 1957). Many of these would be somewhat more fixed or stable than some of the urban places mentioned above. However, notions of sociability would seem to be important aspects of these associations whatever their stated purposes and they are clearly distinct from places of employment or residential neighbourhoods.

Others might be more commercial enterprises such as the espresso bars in England of the 1960s, especially colonized by young people (Moran 2007) or the development of a kind of café culture in new urban villages (Bell and Jayne 2004). But perhaps closest to my typification above is the Speakers' Corner in London's Hyde Park. Davina Cooper describes this space as a 'comedic public space' and refers to the process of 'the constitution and interaction of regulars and strangers' (Cooper 2006: 755). The whole arrangement of speakers, each surrounded by a mixture of regulars and casual visitors seems to facilitate exchanges between speakers and members of the audience and within the audiences themselves.

Many of these sites have been discussed in earlier chapters and I shall refer to one further example, the British post offices, later in this conclusion. However, it can be said that while acquaintances can and do develop anywhere there are particular sites that appear to especially favour their flourishing.

Significance of acquaintances: for individuals and the self

It can be suggested that the significance of acquaintanceship varies according to the life course. Small, pre-school children, have relatively few acquaintances and are probably less likely or able to distinguish between intimates and acquaintances. In the early school years, similarly, the language of friendship and making and breaking of friends is likely to dominate and the notion of acquaintanceship is likely to be relatively undeveloped. In retrospect, perhaps, there were all kinds of acquaintances who were not recognized as such at the time; neighbours, friends of one's parents, school teachers or older pupils and so on. However, perhaps the more significant difference is between intimates and strangers (or friends and enemies) with the notion of acquaintanceship being relatively less well developed.

In later life, various life-course transitions may involve the expansion of the number of acquaintances and with this the development of more complex notions of acquaintanceship. Notions of etiquette, whether formalized or less formal, may be seen as addressing relationships between acquaintances rather than between intimates. Each transition, from school to work, leaving home, into military service (where relevant), higher or further education and so on, brings with it a widening of the range of acquaintances and of the idea of acquaintanceship. Other movements, between jobs or between residences, may have a similar effect.

It might be imagined that retirement and old age bring with them a diminution in the numbers and importance of acquaintances. This is, however, not necessarily the case, especially with the growing significance of older age groups in the population as a whole and the development of a whole range of post-retirement activities.

We can also begin to think about the significance of acquaintanceship at different stages of the life cycle, referring to notions such as social capital, a sense of ontological security and the strength of weak ties. These significances will vary over time and occur in different mixes. However, what needs to be stressed here is the significance of acquaintances in constructing a sense of self and of building up identities over time. In terms of the life that is lived, acquaintances at different times might be useful in providing information about neighbourhoods, services, employment and, more generally, in navigating oneself around within a complex modern society. These more practical considerations are sometimes less likely to be fulfilled by intimates since they tend to share the same social circles and sets of resources. Further, acquaintances may be sources of simple pleasures and of a counterbalancing to the demands of occupational and, it may also be argued, of intimate life.

Acquaintances, therefore, can be seen as important in different aspects of the life that is lived. But they are also important, to use a distinction sometimes made in auto/biographical studies, in the lives that are told, that is, the stories that we tell about ourselves and others and the ways in which these contribute to the construction of selves. If you consider any published autobiography, you will find numerous references to other people. Some – family, friends, lovers – will be clearly classified as intimates. But others, moving in and out of the narrative, sometimes repeatedly or sometimes briefly at particular moments in the life course, also make their appearance and find their way into the index. Sometimes, there will be an element of name dropping involved; these others will be people whom the writer imagines will be known to (acquaintances of) the reader and will therefore be of interest. But others will be recalled because of their particular significance at certain points in a career or because they in some way remain in the memory. Sometimes, they simply form the basis of a good story, one that bears re-telling. Taken individually, these others might seem to be relatively insignificant; taken cumulatively over a significant period of life they may be seen as contributing to the construction of a self. Symbolic interactionism reminds us that selves exist in relation to other selves. But it would be wrong to suppose that these others are always or necessarily 'significant others' or intimates. Acquaintances may also play their part in the life that is told and in the construction of a self.

Consider, at this point, the conventional way in which urban myths are passed on: they are stories told by a friend of a friend. Some more literary ghost stories have this format as well. What this form of a narrative does is to establish a certain distance between story teller and the story told. 'This is what was told to me' by a friend of a friend; you can chose to believe it or not. I am not about to claim any strong sense of authorship, thereby placing my own veracity or reputation on the line. We, the readers or listeners, are better able to appreciate the story as a story.

This particular narrative form, therefore, seems to have a double significance in terms of our discussion of acquaintanceship. The other narrators involved – the 'friends of friends' – are often themselves acquaintances. And the kind of distancing established between story teller and story is in some ways a representation of the idea of acquaintanceship. Instead of the close interweaving of biographies over time we have brief fragmentary insights into other worlds, accomplished through gossip and stories, which enter into individual lives and have their part to play in the construction of selves and identities.

We may stay with the literary references for a little longer and consider acquaintances as being closer, in tone, to short stories rather than to long novels or epic poems. We are afforded brief, fragmentary flashes of other people's lives, their names, their appearance and some particular events. Then they are gone, the story is over. But in many cases, they remain with us and the brevity of the encounter and the distance adds to the poignancy of the acquaintance. The following quotation from Riesman and Watson says something about what I have tried to convey in talking about narratives, acquaintances and identities: 'Interaction between familiars is highly routinized and reiterative; interaction between casuals is much more likely to be creative, exciting and even intimate' (Riesman and Watson 1964: 238).

The social significance of acquaintanceship

Weak ties and personal communities

There are, inevitably, overlaps between the ways in which acquaintances might be important for individuals and the wider social significance of these ties. This is clearly demonstrated when we come to reconsider the argument dealing with the strength of weak ties and associated topics such as social capital, social networks and personal communities.

Granovetter's influential article deals chiefly with the relationships between groups and the kinds of ties that bridge the gap between the macro and the micro (Granovetter 1973). Social structures are not simply made up of clusters of individuals sharing overlapping sets of strong ties but of ties that are in some ways weaker but which cut across and move beyond such clusters. Individuals with weak ties are more likely to move in different social circles and more likely, therefore, to provide the bridging between different groups or levels within society. The spreading of a rumour, for example, is more likely to take place within a set of weak ties. Within a set of strong ties, the rumour gets around quickly but is likely to remain within a relatively limited circle. While Granovetter only fleetingly makes the difference between friends and acquaintances in a footnote (1973: 1372) it is clear that in talking about the strength of weak ties we are also talking about acquaintances.

Within the broader discussion of social networks and social capital, acquaintances occupy a slightly ambiguous position, depending in part on the kind of acquaintance we are talking about. Acquaintances are somewhat less likely to appear in social networks simply because of the ways in which such networks are conventionally constructed, that is by asking an individual to list others that are important to him or her. Yet, as we have argued, acquaintances are more likely to play their part in establishing bridging ties, linking different social worlds. These ties are important to individuals and to the wider fabric of social life. Yet it is also likely to be the case that acquaintances might also constitute some kind of weak bonding ties. This is true for the individuals who are encountered on a regular, perhaps even daily, basis; the workmates, the neighbours, the travelling companions. They may provide potential or dormant bridging ties but on a day-to-day basis, it is these weak bonds that are important.

It is important to stress at this point that these ties of acquaintanceship that we are describing are not simply of importance to individuals, providing them with a sense of ontological security and some resources with which to navigate paths through the complexities of modern society. They are also descriptive of and, in some ways, constitutive of that social ordering itself. Notions of 'personal communities' are important here. This idea developed in recognition of the fact that although one particularly important (often in ideological terms) version of community, one dealing with close-knit ties within identified locations, might be on the wane, an overall sense of community might not be absent. Delanty describes this form of community in these terms: 'Organised more like a network, community today is abstract and lacks visibility and unity, and as a result is more an imagined condition than a symbolically shaped reality based on fixed reference points' (Delanty 2003: 188).

The notion of a 'personal community' might sound like an oxymoron. Surely, it might be argued, any sense of community must include an idea of sharing? The answer of course is that there is still a sense of sharing but this sense does not spread over, and in equal measures, the whole personal community. Sharing takes places within clusters of workmates, of neighbours and participants in leisure activities but does not usually spread across these clusters. Yet these different clusters, plus other more isolated individuals, constitute a personal community. Such a personal community certainly includes intimates, friends and family, but it also includes acquaintances.

Acquaintanceship and social divisions

At various points in my discussion I have raised questions about acquaintanceship and social divisions such as gender, class and ethnicity. The question is not simply one of whether acquaintanceship reflects social divisions; it is also one about the extent to which they reproduce these divisions. Here I shall confine my discussion to issues of class and gender and use these as illustrations of themes that deserve further investigation.

Trollope writes, in one of his 'Palliser' novels: 'It was the fate of the family that, with a world of acquaintance, they had not many friends' (Trollope 1995[1880]: 3). (In passing we might note the use of the word 'acquaintance' rather than 'acquaintances', referring to processes and cultural assumptions rather than an aggregate of individuals.) Trollope is writing about individuals at the highest level of British society at the time. 'Acquaintance' is a necessary adjunct to position, reflecting the social seasons, the salons, the clubs and the constant need for political alliances and stratagems. Individuals within these circles develop skills in remembering names and working out connections. It is not only that friendship becomes very difficult under such circumstances; it can sometimes be quite threatening. Various plot lines within this sequence of novels deal with acquaintances who wish to make friends or who wish to make claims of friendship.

Although Trollope is dealing with the higher echelons of society in the nineteenth century, we have no reason to suppose that this relationship between political power and social status is any the less today. Indeed, it might be greater with global mobilities and worldwide systems of communication. Further we may see this particular patterning in terms of the balance between friends and acquaintances extending to a whole range of professions and executive positions. One only has to think of the global networks of many academics as well as of CEOs. In a world of considerable mobility, weak ties become a necessity. Such ties arise out of the routine assumptions and working practices of those involved in these circles and contribute to reinforcing their power and status.

These processes have their analogues at more local levels. Vidich and Bensman found that the middle classes in Springdale were the most concerned with social activities (Vidich and Bensman 1958: 61) and this kind of finding has been repeated in numerous community studies or studies of participation in voluntary associations. Relative affluence makes possible the participation in a wide range of social activities and the development of a wide range of ties while involvement in local activities demands that individuals make and extend such ties. Such ties are not necessarily confined to the particular community, however. Many members of local elites may be also defined as cosmopolitans with links outside any particular community.

We can contrast this with accounts of more working-class or rural communities (see Frankenberg 1966). Here we are introduced to denser patterns of overlapping relationships of neighbourhood, kinship and friendship. It is doubtful if the word 'acquaintance' is widely used under such circumstances and terms such as 'mates' can blur differences between individuals. One might say there is less room for acquaintances; the differences are between intimates or near intimates and readily identifiable strangers.

This kind of contrast between the open networks of loose ties associated at the higher levels of society and the denser networks within working-class, rural or ethnic communities may be something of a stereotype and it is likely that more and more people will be found somewhere in the middle, enjoying various mixtures of close and weak ties. Nevertheless it can be hypothesized that the higher one's social level, the greater the proportion of acquaintances within ones particular circle or network. Further, these weak ties of acquaintance play a part in the reproduction of social differences within a modern society.

What of gender? In different parts of this discussion I have suggested that men are more likely to have acquaintances than women or, more exactly, that they will have greater proportions of acquaintances within their social networks or circles. This appears to be the case in studies of work, for example, where men's relationships appear, often, to be more segmented and confined to the workplace than those of women. Traditionally, at least, men are more likely to be found in Oldenberg's third places outside the home (Oldenberg 1991). In some cases, indeed (eighteenth-century coffee houses in London, British working men's clubs and Fleet Street pubs in the past) women were excluded from such sites. Even where such formal restrictions have been lifted, third places in Oldenberg's view tend to be gendered, perhaps as some kind of counterbalance to the demands of modern heterosexual coupledom.

There are, of course, all kinds of reasons why the differences between men and women in this respect, as in many other respects, might be weakening. If, for example, there is an association between the mobilities required of many modern forms of employment and the significance of acquaintances, then women will be increasingly affected by these linkages as their working opportunities have changed. Yet it is unlikely that men and women are completely alike in both the numbers of acquaintances they have and the use of the language of acquaintanceship to describe their social networks. The differences continue and appear to be deeply embedded, perhaps reflecting the gendered nature of the idea of 'the social' itself (Marshall and Witz 2004). One line of investigation might be to do with male anxieties about homosexuality or accusations of homosexuality so that the 'distancing' found in acquaintanceships might reflect some deeper concerns.

However, and more optimistically perhaps, the reverse may be true. If acquaintances and the process of acquaintanceship may reinforce and reproduce differences of class and gender (and equally of ethnicity and generation) they may also cut across, if not undermine, such differences. It is perhaps easier to call a member of the opposite sex an acquaintance rather than a friend and global mobilities may cut across some class and ethnic divisions even while they reinforce others. At the very least, acquaintances can provide insights into other worlds and this is a theme that I shall return to later.

The changing significance of acquaintanceship

In considering the social significance of acquaintanceship it is important to return to the question as to whether acquaintances are more numerous now than at some time in the past. We are talking both in relative and absolute terms here. The overall proportions of acquaintances, relative to intimates, may have grown and the total field of acquaintances might have grown as well.

Throughout this study, at various points, the assumption has been that acquaintances have become more numerous, relatively and absolutely, and that acquaintanceship has become more significant. But over what period? Narratives of change within sociological analysis frequently deal, explicitly or implicitly, with a variety of overlapping time periods. The grander narratives, reflected in the classic tradition of analysis, deal with some kind of comparison between pre-industrial or traditional society and industrial society or some variation on these dualistic reference points. Slightly more modest comparisons might take something like the ending of the Second World War as a point of departure. Others may deal more immediately in the analysis of postmodern, risk or information societies.

These are complex matters but, fortunately, they are of less importance since, as far as acquaintanceship is concerned, the indicators seem to be pointing more or less in the same way. More immediate changes associated with late modernity are folded into longer periods of transformation. Consider the following:

the structure of organizational careers, the opportunities and constraints of the labour market and the complexity of accommodating multiple earners [which] is bound to create a degree of involuntary mobility hand-in-hand with the consequent disruption of significant sets of social relationships.

(Pahl and Pevalin 2005: 437)

Pahl and Pevalin are writing about influences on friendship networks here but their analysis could be extended to acquaintances. Here they are focussing on changes within the labour market and occupational careers together with the associated impact of social and geographical mobilities. Most of these influences have deep structural roots although also have their more contemporary manifestations. In very general terms, the approach identified with Norbert Elias might be a useful point of departure:

as bonds of co-operation and competition between people expanded and intensified, and hierarchical differences between individuals and groups diminished, more people pressured each other to take more of each other into account more often.

(Wouters 2001: 58)

This is at a very general level and some slightly more specific influences, implied by this general orientation, may be listed briefly, as follows:

- The changing nature of work and occupations: employment outside the home, as we have seen, inevitably brings relative strangers together and turns them into acquaintances. We may be talking about workmates, colleagues or clients. The cultivation of acquaintances may be required (in politics and some professions) or may be a consequence of the work.
- The growth of service occupations, especially those requiring emotional or aesthetic labour, increases the numbers of others who are encountered on a day-to-day basis.
- Whether or not social mobility has increased remains a complex matter. However it seems likely that, for some at least, there have been increases in occupational and geographical mobility. This almost inevitably means a rise in the number and proportion of acquaintances even for those whose personal mobility is relatively modest since others will also be moving into their social field. This applies both to the workplace and to residential areas where there are flows in and out.
- We may add to this the intensification of urban life, affecting not only employment but also consumption and leisure.
- Part of this is reflected and reinforced by the growth of transport systems whether they be more locally based metro or bus systems or international air travel.
- Developments in systems of communication, especially the Internet, also contribute to the expansion of the field of acquaintances, at least potentially,

This is an open-ended list and purely designed to show the multiple influences likely to increase the numbers, relatively and absolutely, of acquaintances.

Are there any countervailing tendencies? It might be suggested that the growth of forms of domestic privatization, where the nexus of intimate relationships associated with home and family become more important, perhaps act as a counter-balance to the changes taking place in occupational life and labour markets. The theme of the home as a haven in a heartless world has become a popular one in sociological analysis and some evidence may be produced to support it. In addition, and more generally, we may note arguments that stress the importance of intimate relationships as a whole; relationships which individuals have to work at and which are a source of mutual support, confiding and multi-stranded intimacies. These intimacies extend beyond 'conventional' heterosexual marital or family relationships to include diverse sexualities and friendships. Some of these intimate relationships may be short lived but this does not diminish their importance. Indeed, the very vulnerability of such relationships may increase their desirability. In such a context, acquaintances may not disappear – indeed they are inevitable – but their significance might be severely reduced.

It is difficult to evaluate these two, rather loose, models, the one arguing for an increase in acquaintances with the other stressing the growing importance of intimacy. It might seem rather feeble to conclude that both are possible but this can be supported on at least two grounds. The first is to suggest that the various balances between acquaintances and intimates might vary, as has already been suggested, according to life course and to social divisions such as age, gender, social class and ethnicity. The other is to make a distinction between the number of acquaintances and their significance to the individual. As has already been noted, acquaintances have an ascribed character; they are there whether we like them or not. The question is less one of whether we have acquaintances but of how we relate to them. And this, in some measure, brings us to questions of ethics.

Acquaintanceship and public life

In talking about the distinctions between intimates and acquaintances we are, to some extent, talking about the differences between the private and the public. Acquaintances are, generally speaking, more likely to be found in the public sphere. We have seen that this becomes a difficult distinction, especially when we think about places of employment, but it represents a useful approximation for the present purposes.

The argument can be taken a step further. It can be suggested that acquaintances contribute to the quality of public life. This is very much the argument of Oldenberg in his discussion of 'third places' (1991). Third places can provide not only a broadening of perspective but a different kind of perspective, 'a disinterest impossible in home and work settings' (p. 51). Somewhat similar claims may be found in Keane's discussion of 'micro-public spheres' (Keane: 1995/2004: 368):

> Such public spheres as the discussion circle, the publishing house, the church, the clinic, and a political chat over a drink with friends or acquaintances are the sites in which citizens question the

pseudo-imperatives of reality and counter them with alternative experiences of time, space and interpersonal relations.

Public life, therefore, is more than particular physical spaces and it is even more than the people who may be found in such spaces. It is the way in which people within such spaces relate to each other and to the wider social and political contexts within which they find themselves. As an illustration, I shall refer to debates currently taking place in Britain, about the future of local post offices.

As I write, some 2500 local post offices up and down the country are under threat of closure (Barkham 2008). Accounts of such places describe not only the use of various services provided by these offices (collecting pensions, buying stamps or posting parcels) but a whole host of informal services provided above and beyond these and numerous small but repeated social interactions. The individuals who run these offices accumulate considerable knowledge about their customers and can 'look out' for them if, for example, they fail to pick up their pension. Similarly, people on the way to the post office will encounter others engaged in similar errands, so that a complex micro-world of acquaintanceship may be established.

Now that such places are under threat, responses to possible closures can intensify the sense of public life. Petitions will be signed and protests mounted and these activities can give greater depths to these networks of acquaintances. In the course of expressing their anxieties, individuals may elaborate ideas about the position of the elderly in society, differences between rural and urban life or more simply the distinction between 'them' and 'us'. Keane's phrase about the question of 'pseudo-imperatives' seems to be especially apt here and in other similar locally based protests. We are dealing not simply with relations in public but with the reproduction of public life as something to be valued.

The ethics of acquaintanceship

If the notion of a public sphere or public life means anything it is something to do with the relationships that we have with others who are not our intimates. Indeed it can be argued that there is something limiting about sets of social relationships that consist almost wholly of intimates and certainly the ethical content of public life begins where these intimate circles end.

If we look at intimates, friends and family, our ethical commitments are defined in terms of obligations, however much these may be open to negotiation in practice (Finch 1989; Finch and Mason 1993). Where ethical obligations towards strangers are defined these are more likely to be expressed in terms of codes, formal or informal, referring to questions such as hospitality. Major religious traditions all have something to say as to how we should treat strangers. In contrast to these two spheres, intimates and strangers, acquaintances seem to be less ethically charged.

However, acquaintances are not ethically neutral. In the first place the knowledge that individuals have of each other also can involve an element of recognition (Sayer 2005: 52–69). This is a stronger and more complex idea than simply possessing knowledge of the other. It is a recognition of the other as someone who is both distinct from ourselves but also alike. These ethical concerns recur frequently in the writings of Goffman on interpersonal interaction and relations in public.

Second, and linked to this, relationships with acquaintances belong in the sphere of what has been described as 'quotidian ethics', 'the morality of our small, everyday interactions with other people' (Baggini, quoted in Truss, 2006: 15). Such ethical practices are less likely to be elaborated in moral codes or to deal with the great issues of life and death, pain and vulnerability. They are more likely to evolve over time and to be elaborated and implicitly negotiated in everyday exchanges and encounters. They may be linked, ultimately, to notions of human embodiment and selfhood but these deeper matters rarely come to the fore in these everyday meetings of acquaintances.

There are links here with the idea of etiquette. It is interesting that there has, since the late 1990s, been a revival of interest in etiquette, at least in Britain, seeing these as something more than outdated sets of rules relating to polite society. It may be the development of a whole host of novel situations associated with say, mobile telephones, the use of email, the cultural complexities of modern societies not simply in terms of nationality and ethnicity but also in terms of matters to do with sexualities, that has stimulated this revival of interest. Etiquette seems to be centrally concerned with relationships between acquaintances rather than those between intimates where other considerations arise.

This takes us back to the weakly ascribed character of acquaintanceship. Acquaintances occur 'naturally' in the course of everyday living in a complex world. We do not normally choose them and they do not have the deep ascriptive quality of some intimate relations. Yet we can chose how to 'do' acquaintanceship. This involves some degree of transcending the immediate, often instrumental, character of such as ascribed acquaintances and recognizing the other through a variety of bodily and linguistic practices. At the same time there is a recognition of the limitations of this transcending of the merely instrumental. The ethics of acquaintanceship, as has been noted so often, is to do with the delicate balancing between distance and intimacy.

In this section I have dealt largely with everyday, interpersonal, ethics and how these shape and are shaped by the ways in which people respond to each other in encounters outside the spheres of home and friends. But there is also another aspect of this dealing with the extent to which acquaintanceship can broaden our moral horizons and sympathies.

Within immediate circles of friends and family there are ongoing sets of ties and obligations. Many of these have well established roots and are based upon intertwining biographies and supported by widespread notions of the value of friends, family and intimate relations. Within such a framework there may often be some ambivalences but this does not detract from the strength and the centrality of such ties in many people's lives. They are the 'significant others', the persons most likely to be placed within the inner circles of every widening relationships. These are the 'ties that bind'.

The value of such ties has been frequently stated and explored and it is also the case that some such ties can lead to a widening of sympathies. This may occur as a consequence of marriages outside ones immediate social circle, for example, or of social and geographical mobility. Very often, however, these ties can be limiting and containing, especially where they exist within a wider community context. Acquaintances, in contrast, can extend our knowledge and understandings beyond the routinized taken-for granted frameworks that emerge within networks of intimate ties. Such an extension of sympathies beyond the immediate is, as Sen and others have argued, essential for coming to grips with a complex and diverse world (Sen 2006).

One idea linked to this extension of moral sympathies and understandings beyond the immediacies of kin and friends is that of 'cosmopolitanism'. In Merton's use of the word, cosmopolitans were contrasted with locals and referred to those whose reference groups and social networks extended beyond the boundaries of an immediate community (Merton 1957). More recent usages extend this notion and frequently stress the ethical dimensions of cosmopolitan orientations (e.g. Werbner 2008). Binnie and Skeggs, in an article dealing with Manchester's 'gay village', stress the dimension of knowledge: 'To be a cosmopolitan one has to have access to a particular form of knowledge, able to appropriate and know the other and generate authority from this knowing' (Binnie and Skeggs 2004: 42).

Of course, such knowledge can have its limitations. It may be quite superficial, perhaps even stereotypical. It may be limited to people within social circles whose characteristics are very similar to those of ones more immediate intimate circles. Yet it may also promote an understanding that while the others we encounter at work, in our neighbourhoods or more casually may be different from us in all kinds of ways they may also be more alike, more than we might suspect, in other ways. This kind of understanding is well expressed by Saul Bellow in speaking of his assumed readership: 'I have in mind another human being who will understand me. I count on this. Not on perfect understanding, which is Cartesian, but on approximate understanding, which is Jewish. And on a meeting of sympathies, which is human' (*Paris Review* 2007: 98).

Acquaintanceship and everyday life

The main emphasis throughout this discussion has been at the more individual or interpersonal level, assessing the significance of acquaintanceship for individuals as they go about their daily lives. But the significance can also be assessed in more societal terms and here I want to consider the ways in which acquaintanceship may be seen as contributing to a construction of the 'everyday'.

One of sociology's main achievements has been the way in which it has problematized the everyday and rendered the routine, the taken-for-granted, as mysterious and strange. Numerous writers have contributed to this sense of the social construction of everyday life and knowledge – Berger and Luckmann, Goffman, Simmel, Lefebvre, Schutz and several others – and this is not the place to provide a detailed account of these insights. Instead I shall take a useful discussion by Felski (1999/2000) and attempt to apply this to my study of acquaintanceship.

She writes:

> I want to piece together an alternative definition of everyday life grounded in three key facets: time, space and modality. The temporality of the everyday, I suggest, is that of repetition, the spatial ordering of the everyday is anchored in a sense of home and the characteristic mode of experiencing the everyday is that of habit.
>
> (Felski 1999/2000: 18)

To begin with repetition. Many of the activities which generate acquaintances are to do with the regularities of modern life. Leaving home at the same time, seeing more or less the same people at one's place of employment, meeting or seeing the same people in the journey between home and work as well as the regularities associated with weekends and holidays: all these and more constitute the temporal basis of acquaintanceship. For women, given the persistence of gendered divisions of labour within the home, these regularities might include trips to the shops, to the school to kin or neighbours. From the point of view of this study it is not the simple fact of routines and regularities which are important but the fact that these routines necessarily involve interactions with and the accumulation of knowledge about others. The association between repetition and everyday life is essentially a relational one, built up through acquaintances.

Here one may note, to use a term developed by Sartre, the seriality of these relationships (Craib 1976). The others encountered through the repetitions of everyday life are not usually strongly linked to each other. At best they constitute a loose-knit network from the perspective of the individual. Put another way, it is not necessary that they have these other close linkages although, from time to time, such connections may exist and reveal themselves. (This is part of the 'small world' phenomenon.) One of the consequences of this is the potential diversity of these others, encountered in these repetitions, so that everyday life is more like a patchwork quilt or a mosaic over which the eye may stray, building up numerous connections or stories.

Turning to 'home', the facet of space, it might appear that this is more normally seen as the sphere of the intimate rather than of acquaintanceship. Certainly there would seem to be a strong tendency in modern societies to see home in terms of the significant others within it (Holdsworth and Morgan 2006). Home may certainly contribute to a sense of the everyday but this is achieved largely through ongoing interactions with intimates.

But this may be to adopt too limited, and it might be said, too contemporary a sense of home. A sense of home is not only built up, internally, through interactions with significant others, but also externally through its existence within a locality or neighbourhood. To 'go home' is not simply to be greeted within the walls of a particular dwelling but to walk along familiar streets, passing familiar landmarks. And within these spatial familiarities we find acquaintances. Home is not simply a nexus of close interdependencies but it is also a basis from which to move out into the wider neighbourhood and to renew old acquaintances.

Of course, from the perspective of acquaintanceship, the facet of space need not, indeed cannot, be confined to the home, even in this somewhat expanded understanding. We have seen how the spatialities of work and urban life have contributed to the development of acquaintances and it is important to be reminded that acquaintances are always acquaintances in space. Thus it may not always be the case that we expect to see the same people in the same places. However it is one of our expectations that we expect to see similar people – shop assistants, taxi drivers, waiters – in similar places and it is through these routinized expectations that we build up a sense of everyday life.

Habit in some ways seems to be close to repetition although it refers more to the orientations of the actor rather than to the actual practices. Habit is a mode of being in the world that does not routinely call into question the evident dimensions of that world. Habit builds up and reproduces a sense of the everyday and the taken-for-granted: 'In other words, everyday life is the sphere of what Schutz calls the natural attitude' (Felski 1999/2000: 27).

What needs to be stressed is that these habits do not simply belong to the individual actor. Purely individual habits come closer to fetishistic obsessions. Habit requires the unspoken and unrecognized cooperations of others as we go about our daily business. These others are more likely than not to be acquaintances. Intimates, indeed, may be more likely to call into question the habits of their significant others. It makes sense to ask 'what is your partner's most annoying habit?' It makes less sense to ask this of many of the acquaintances we have met in the course of this book.

This discussion has been a series of riffs stimulated by Felski's article rather than an elaborated theoretical exposition. The core argument has been that acquaintances are part of the process of building up a sense of the everyday in time, space, practices and orientations to the world. We see this as essentially a cooperative if serialized process through which the everyday is affirmed and reproduced on a regular basis.

But these pieces, these individually insignificant others, do not necessarily fit together to form a coherent whole. Rather than constituting a complete jigsaw puzzle they resemble a loose assemblage based upon the pieces of several incomplete jigsaw puzzles. Therein lies the fascination of acquaintanceship and their potentialities for overcoming the particularities of intimacy and opening up, if only fleetingly, new worlds.

Final remarks: acquaintanceship and sociological practice

Sociologists, like anyone else, have acquaintances. In common with most other people they have acquaintances based upon where they live and as a consequence of conducting the everyday errands of social life. They have acquaintances based upon where they work and this has two dimensions. These are the people encountered, sociologists and non-sociologists, in the actual locations of their employment, the universities and research institutes. But they also have acquaintances based upon wider professional networks and encountered in conferences, in visiting lectures or temporary employment.

To this extent, sociologists have a lot in common with members of many other professions. But they also have another link to our themes in that many of the everyday practices of research require the making of acquaintances and the elaboration of acquaintanceship. This is, of course, especially the case with qualitative research involving participant observation or interviews. Some of these research subjects may come to be defined as friends, as several researchers have testified. But most of them will be acquaintances and the knowledge that we have of them or derive from them will be the basis of our enquiries. The kinds of debates that sociologists have around the ethics of these encounters revolve partly around issues of exploitation and partly about achieving a working balance between intimacy and distance. It should be noted that the concerns here go in two directions. It is not simply in terms of what knowledge we gain about and from our informants and the limitations surrounding this knowledge and the questions that are asked. It is also to do with the knowledge about ourselves that we supply to our informants, both directly in terms of what we say about ourselves and indirectly in terms of the information that is given off by our appearance and bodily demeanour.

This deployment of acquaintanceship is, of course, most marked in ethnographic and qualitative research and most muted in more quantitative modes of sociological enquiry. It can also exist in archival or historical research where persons from the past can take on the character of acquaintances (much like fictional characters) or, sometimes, even intimates. What I am suggesting here is that there is a close affinity between the conduct of social enquiry and our overall theme of acquaintanceship. This does not stop with the actual research. In conference presentations or published papers, the acquaintances gained in the source of qualitative research also, in some lesser and more fleeting way, become the acquaintances of those who read or hear about the particular research project.

Thus a consideration of acquaintanceship, which I have argued is a proper subject for social enquiry, brings us back to the research process itself. And this should not be a surprise. We cannot avoid acquaintances; they are an inevitable, and I would argue an increasing, part of modern life. What we have some control over is the use that we make of these acquaintances, these others, and the ways in which they enlarge our understanding whether as sociologists or, more generally, as citizens and members of a global society.

References

Ackroyd, P. (1990) *Dickens*. London: Sinclair-Stevenson.
Ackroyd, S. and Thompson, P. (1999) *Organizational Misbehaviour*. London: Sage.
Adam, B. (1998) *Timescapes of Modernity: The Environment and Invisible Hazards*. London: Routledge.
Archer, M. (2003) *Structure, Agency and the Internal Conversation*. Cambridge: Cambridge University Press.
Argyle, K. and Shields, R. (1996) 'Is there a body in the net?' in R. Shields (ed.) *Cultures of Internet: Virtual Spaces, Real Histories, Living Bodies*. London: Sage.
Bain, A. (2005) 'Constructing an artistic identity', *Work, Employment and Society*, 19(1): 25–46.
Barkham, P. (2008) The last post protest, *Guardian*, 9 April.
Barthes, R. (1972) *Mythologies*. London: Cape.
Bell, D. and Jayne, M. (eds) (2004) *City of Quarters: Urban Villages in the Contemporary City*. Aldershot: Ashgate.
Benedict, J. (1997) *Public Heroes, Private Felons: Athletes and Crimes Against Women*. Boston: Northeastern University Press.
Benedict, J.R. (1998) *Athletes and Acquaintances Rape*. Thousand Oaks, CA: Sage
Berger, P.L. and Luckmann, T. (1967) *The Social Construction of Reality: A Treatise in the Sociology of Knowledge*. Harmondsworth: Penguin.
Bergmann, J.R. (1993) *Discreet Indiscretions: The Social Organization of Gossip*. New York: Transaction Publications.
Bindel, J. (2005) 'The life stealers', *Guardian Weekend*, 16 April.
Binnie, J. and Skeggs, B. (2004) 'Cosmopolitan knowledge and the production and consumption of sexualized space: Manchester's gay village', *Sociological Review*, 52(1): 39–61.
Bishop, V., Korczynski, M. and Cohen, L. (2005) 'The invisibility of violence: constructing violence out of the job centre workplace in the UK', *Work, Employment and Society*, 19(3): 583–602.
Blokland, T. (2003) *Urban Bonds*. Cambridge: Polity Press.
Bone, J. (2006) *The Hard Sell: An Ethnographic Study of the Direct Selling Industry*. Aldershot: Ashgate.
Bradley, H. (2000) *Myths at Work*. Cambridge: Polity.
Brandth, B. and Haugen, M.S. (2005) Farmers as tourist hosts. Consequences for work and identity. Paper presented to the European Society for Rural Sociology XXIst Congress, Kerszthely, Hungary, 22–27 August.
Brannan, M.J. (2005) 'Once more with feeling: ethnographic reflections on the mediation

of tension in a small team of call centre workers', *Gender, Work and Organization*, 12(5): 420–39.
Bridge, G. and Watson, S. (eds) (2002) *The Blackwell City Reader*. Oxford: Blackwell.
Bury, M. and Gabe, J. (eds) (2004) *The Sociology of Health and Illness: A Reader*. London: Routledge.
Cain, M. (1983) 'The general practice lawyer and the client: towards a radical conception', in R. Dingwall and P. Lewis (eds) *The Sociology of the Professions: Lawyers, Doctors and Others*. London: Macmillan/SSRC.
Cavan, S. (1973) 'Bar sociability', in A. Birenbaum and E. Sagarin (eds) *People in Places: The Sociology of the Familiar*. London: Nelson.
Cavendish, R. (1982) *Women on the Line*. London: Routledge & Kegan Paul.
Collinson, D.L. (1992) *Managing the Shopfloor: Subjectivity, Masculinity and Workplace Culture*. Berlin: De Gryter.
Cooper, D. (2006) '"Sometimes a community and sometimes a battlefield": from the comedic public space to the commons of Speakers' Corner', *Environmental and Planning D: Society and Space*, 24: 753–75.
Coulthard, M. and Ashby, M. (1976) 'A linguistic description of doctor-patient interviews', in M. Wadsworth and D. Robinson (eds) *Studies in Everyday Medical Life*. London: Martin Robertson.
Craib, I. (1976) *Existentialism and Sociology: A Study of Jean-Paul Sartre*. Cambridge: Cambridge University Press.
Crow, G. and Allan, G. (1994) *Community Life: An Introduction to Local Social Relations*. Hemel Hempstead: Harvester/Wheatsheaf.
Crow, G., Allan, G. and Summers, M. (2002) 'Neither busybodies nor nobodies: managing proximity and distance in neighbourly relations', *Sociology*, 36(1): 127–45.
Dalton, M. (1959) *Men who Manage*. New York: John Wiley.
Damer, S. (1989) *From Moorepark to 'Wine Alley': The Rise and Fall of a Glasgow Housing Scheme*. Edinburgh: Edinburgh University Press.
Davis, A. and Horobin, G. (eds) (1977) *Medical Encounters: The Experience of Illness and Treatment*. London: Croom Helm.
Davis, F. (1959) 'The cabdriver and his fare: facets of a fleeting relationship', *American Journal of Sociology*, 65: 160–6.
Davis, M.S. (1973) *Intimate Relations*. New York: The Free Press.
Delanty, G. (2003) *Community*. London: Routledge.
Dennis, N., Henriques, F. and Slaughter, C. (1956) *Coal Is Our Life*. London: Eyre & Spottiswoode.
Dyer, R. (2004) *Heavenly Bodies: Film Stars and Society, 2nd edn*. London: Routledge.
Elias, N. (1970) *What is Sociology?* London: Hutchinson.
Elias, N. (1987) *Involvement and Detachment*. Oxford: Basil Blackwell.
Elias, N. (1991) *The Society of Individuals*. Oxford: Basil Blackwell.
Elias, N. (1998) *On Civilization, Power and Knowledge: Selected Writings* (Ed. S. Mennell and J. Goudsblom). Chicago: University of Chicago Press.
Eyres, H. (2005) Beyond toil: an ineffable humanity, *The Financial Times*, 24 September.
Fairhurst, E. (1977) 'On being a patient in an orthopaedic ward: some thoughts on the definition of the situation', in A. Davis and G. Horobin (eds) *Medical Encounters: The Experiences of Illness and Treatment*. London: Croom Helm.
Felski, R. (1999/2000) 'The invention of everyday life', *New Formations*, 39: 13–31.
Finch, E. (2001) *The Criminalisation of Stalking: Constructing the Problem and Evaluating the Solution*. London: Cavendish Publishing Ltd.
Finch, J. (1989) *Family Obligations and Social Change*. Cambridge: Polity Press.
Finch, J. and Mason, J. (1993) *Negotiating Family Responsibilities*. London: Routledge.
Fineman, S. (2003) *Understanding Emotions at Work*. London: Sage.

Firth, R. (1977) 'Routines in a tropical diseases hospital', in A Davis and G. Horobin (eds) *Medical Encounters: The Experiences of Illness and Treatment*. London: Croom Helm.
Fiske, J. (1992) 'The cultural economy of fandom', in A.L. Lewis (ed.) *The Adoring Audience: Fan Culture and Popular Media*. London: Routledge.
Forseth, U. (2005) 'Gender matters? Exploring how gender is negotiated in service encounters', *Gender, Work and Organization*, 12(5): 440–59.
Fox, K. (2004) *Watching the English: The Hidden Rules of English Behaviour*. London: Hodder.
Frankenberg, R. (1957) *Village on the Border*. London: Cohen & West.
Frankenberg, R. (1966) *Communities in Britain*. Harmondsworth: Penguin.
Frisby, D. (1992) *Simmel and Since: Essays on Georg Simmel's Social Theory*. London: Routledge.
Frost, R. (1928/1951) *Complete Poems*. London: Cape.
Gans, H.J. (1965) *The Urban Villagers: Group and Class in the Life of Italian Americans*. New York: The Free Press.
Gans, H.J. (1967) *The Levittowners: Ways of Life and Politics in a New Suburban Community*. London: Allen Lane, The Penguin Press.
Giddens, A. (1992) *The Transformation of Intimacy: Sexuality, Love and Eroticism in Modern Societies*. Cambridge: Polity Press.
Gluckman, M. (1963) 'Gossip and scandal', *Current Anthropology*, iv: 307–16.
Goffman, E. (1963) *Behaviour in Public Places: Notes on the Social Organization of Gatherings*. New York: The Free Press.
Goffman, E. [1961] (1968) *Asylums: Essays on the Social Situations of Mental Patients and Other Inmates*. Harmondsworth: Penguin.
Goffman, E. (1971) *Relations in Public*. London: Allen Lane, The Penguin Press.
Goffman, E. (1983) 'The interaction order', *American Sociological Review*, 48: 1–17.
Goldthorpe, J.H., Lockwood, D., Bechofer, F. and Platt, J. (1968) *The Affluent Worker: Industrial Attitudes and Behaviour*. Cambridge: Cambridge University Press.
Gouldner, A.W. (1955) *Patterns of Industrial Bureaucracy*. London: Routledge & Kegan Paul.
Granovetter, M. (1973) 'The strength of weak ties', *American Journal of Sociology*, 78: 1360–80.
Gurney, C. (2000) 'Transgressing public/private boundaries in the home: a sociological analysis of the coital noise taboo', *Venerology*, 13: 39–46.
Gustavsson, E. (2005) 'Virtual servants: stereotyping female front-office employees on the internet', *Gender, Work and Organization*, 12(5): 400–19.
Haavio-Mannila, E. (1998) 'Attractions and love at work', in D. Von der Fehr, B. Rosenbeck and A.G. Jonasdottir (eds) *Is There a Nordic Feminism? Nordic Feminist Thought on Culture and Society*. London: UCL Press.
Hague, F. (2008) *The Pain and the Privilege: The Women in Lloyd George's Life*. London: Harperpress.
Hamilton, P. [1947] (2006) *The Slaves of Solitude*. London: Constable.
Hanley, L. (2008) *Estates: An Intimate History*. London: Granta Books.
Hannerz, U. (1969) *Soulside: Inquiries into Ghetto Culture and Community*. New York: Columbia University Press.
Haugen, I. and Holtedahl, L. (1982) 'Regulating togetherness', *Acta Sociologica*, 25: 3–20.
Heath, C. (1981) 'The opening sequence in doctor-patient interaction', in P. Atkinson and C. Heath (eds) *Medical Work: Realities and Routines*. Farnborough: Gower.
Heath, S. (2004) 'Peer-shared households, quasi-communes and neo tribes', *Current Sociology*, 52(2): 161–79.
Highsmith, P. (1999) *The Cry of the Owl*. New York: Vintage.

Hochschild, A.R. (1983) *The Managed Heart: Commercialization of Human Feelings.* Berkeley, CA: University of California Press.
Holdsworth, C. and Morgan, D. (2005) *Transitions in Context: Leaving Home, Independence and Adulthood.* Maidenhead: Open University Press.
Homans, G. (1951) *The Human Group.* London: Routledge & Kegan Paul.
Hughes, E.C. (1971) *The Sociological Eye: Selected Papers.* Chicago: Aldine.
Hugman, R. (2005) *New Approaches in Ethics for the Caring Professions.* Basingstoke: Palgrave Macmillan.
Independent Extra (2007) 'Who's listening? The people at the other end of Britain's helplines', 4 May.
Jacobs, J. [1961] (1969) *The Death and Life of Great American Cities.* New York: The Modern Library.
Jamieson, L. (1998) *Intimacy: Personal Relationships in Modern Societies.* Cambridge: Polity.
Jeffries, S. (2007) 'Hi Stu, you don't know me but . . . big hug! XXX', *Guardian*, 26 June.
Jenkins, H. (1992) *Textual Poachers: Television Fame and Participatory Culture.* New York and London: Routledge.
Johnson, B. (2006) 'One in ten teenagers say they are victims of the rise of cyberbullies', *Guardian*, 15 March.
Jonze, T. (2006) 'Death on Myspace', *Guardian*, 15 May.
Kamir, O. (2001) *Every Breath You Take: Stalking Narratives and the Law.* Ann Arbor, MI: University of Michigan Press.
Katz, F.E. (1968) *Autonomy and Organization: The Limits of Social Control.* New York: Random House.
Keane, J. [1995] (2004) 'Structural transformations of the public sphere', in F. Webster (ed.) *The Information Society Reader.* London: Routledge.
Kenyon, L. (1999) 'A home from home: students' transitional experiences of home', in T. Chapman and J. Hockey (eds.) *Ideal Homes? Social Change and Domestic Life.* London: Routledge.
Lang, G.E. and Lang, K. (1988) 'Recognition and renown: the survival of artistic reputation', *American Journal of Sociology*, 94(1): 79–109.
Lefebvre, H. (2004) *Rhythmanalysis: Space, Time and Everyday Life.* London: Continuum.
Lemert, C.C. and Branaman, A (eds) (1997) *The Goffman Reader.* Cambridge, MA: Blackwell.
Letherby, G. and Reynolds, G. (2005) *Train Tracks: Work, Play and Politics on the Railway.* Oxford: Berg.
Lewis, L.A. (ed.) (1992) *The Adoring Audience: Fan Culture and Popular Media.* London: Routledge.
Lewis, P. (2005) 'Suppression or expression: and exploration of emotions management in a special care baby unit', *Work, Employment and Society*, 19(3): 565–82.
Littler, J. (2004) 'Celebrity and meritocracy', *Soundings*, 26: 118–30.
Lofland, J. (1966) *Doomsday Cult: A Study of Conversion, Proselytization and Maintenance of Faith.* Englewood Cliffs, NJ: Prentice Hall.
Lofland, L.A. (1973) *A World of Strangers: Order and Action in Urban Public Space.* New York: Basic Books.
Low, S.M. (2002) 'Spatializing culture: the social construction of public space in Costa Rica', in G. Bridge and S. Watson (eds) *The Blackwell City Reader.* Oxford: Blackwell.
Lupton, D. (2003) *Medicine as Culture: Illness, Disease and the Body in Western Societies.* London: Sage.
Lury, C. (1998) *Prosthetic Culture: Photography, Memory and Identity.* London: Routledge.
Macdonald, K.M. (1995) *The Sociology of the Professions.* London: Sage.
McEwan, I. (1997) *Enduring Love.* London: Cape.

Marshall, B.L. and Witz, A. (eds) (2004) *Engendering the Social: Feminist Encounters with Sociological Theory*. Maidenhead: Open University Press.
Marshall, P. D. (1997) *Celebrity and Power: Fame in Contemporary Culture*. Minneapolis: University of Minnesota Press.
Melbin, M. (1987) *Night as Frontier*. New York: The Free Press.
Mennell, S. and Goudsblom, J. (1998) Introduction to N. Elias *On Civilization, Power and Knowledge: Selected Writings*. Chicago: University of Chicago Press.
Merton, R. K. (1957) *Social Theory and Social Structure* (revised enlarged edition). Glencoe, Illinois: The Free Press.
Mills, C.W. (1956) *White Collar: The American Middle Classes*. New York: Galaxy Books.
Moran, J. (2007) *Queuing for Beginners: The Story of Daily Life from Breakfast to Bedtime*. London: Profile Books.
Morgan, D. (1969) Theoretical and conceptual problems in the study of social relations at work: an analysis of differing definitions of women's roles in a northern factory. Unpublished PhD thesis, University of Manchester.
Morgan, D. (1982) 'Cultural work and friendship work: the case of "Bloomsbury"', *Media, Culture and Society*, 4: 19–32.
Morgan, D. (1987) *'It Will Make a Man of You': Notes on National Service, Masculinity and Autobiography*. University of Manchester Studies in Sexual Politics No. 17.
Morgan, D. (1996) *Family Connections: An Introduction to Family Studies*. Cambridge: Polity Press.
Morgan, D. (2004) 'Everyday life and family practices', in E.B. Silva and T. Bennett (eds) *Contemporary Culture and Everyday Life*. Durham: sociologypress.
Morgan, D. (2005) 'Revisiting "Communities in Britain"', *Sociological Review*, 53(4): 641–57.
Morgan, D. (2008) 'Are community studies still "good to think with?"', in R. Edwards (ed.) *Researching Families and Communities: Social and Generational Change*. London: Routledge.
Mulgan, G. and Burdett, R. (2005) 'What makes a good neighbour?', *RSA Journal*, December: 56–9.
Nettleton, S. (1995) *The Sociology of Health and Illness*. Cambridge: Polity Press.
Newcomb, T. M. (1961) *The Acquaintance Process*. New York: Holt, Rinehard & Winston.
Oldenburg, R. (1991) *The Great Good Place*. New York: Paragon House.
Pahl, R. and Pevalin, D.J. (2005) 'Between family and friends: a longitudinal study of friendship choice', *British Journal of Sociology*, 56(3): 433–50.
Paris Review, The (2007) *The Paris Review Interviews, Vol. 1*. Edinburgh: Canongate.
Perren, K., Arber, S. and Davidson, K. (2004) 'Neighbouring in later life: the influence of socio-economic resources, gender and household composition in neighbourly relationships', *Sociology*, 38(5): 965–84.
Pettinger, L. (2005) 'Friends, relations and colleagues: the blurred boundaries of the workplace', in L. Pettinger, J. Parry, R. Taylor and M. Glucksmann (eds) *A New Sociology of Work?* Oxford: Blackwell.
Pettinger, L., Parry, J., Taylor, R. and Glucksmann, M. (eds) (2005) *A New Sociology of Work?* Oxford: Blackwell.
Pollert, A. (1981) *Girls, Wives, Factory Lives*. London: Palgrave Macmillan.
Porter, M. (1983) *Home and Work and Class Consciousness*. Manchester: Manchester University Press.
Rasmussen, B. (2005) 'Gut feeling, back-slapping – gendered embodiment on the exchange', in D. Morgan, B. Brandth and E. Kvande (eds) *Gender, Bodies and Work*. Aldershot: Ashgate.
Rayner, J. (2007) Interview with Sean McDermott, doorman, *Observer Magazine* 28 January.

Renner, R.G. (1990) *Edward Hopper, 1882–1967: Transformation of the Real*. Koln: Benedikt Taschen.
Richman, J. (1983) *Traffic Wardens: An Ethnography of Street Administration*. Manchester: Manchester University Press.
Riesman, D. (1961) *The Lonely Crowd: A Study of Changing American Character*. New Haven: Yale University Press.
Riesman, D. and Watson, J. (1964) 'The sociability project: a chronicle of frustration and achievement', in P.E. Hammond (ed.) *Sociologists at Work*. New York: Basic Books.
Roethlisberger, F.J. and Dickson, W.J. (1939) *Management and the Worker*. Cambridge, MA: Harvard University Press.
Rojek, C. (2001) *Celebrities*. London: Reaktion Books.
Roper, M. (1994) *Masculinity and the British Organization Man Since 1945*. Oxford: Oxford University Press.
Roy, D.F. (1960) ' "Banana time": job satisfaction and informal interaction', *Human Organization*, XIII: 158–68.
Sanders, W.B. (1973) 'Pinball occasions', in A. Birenbaum and E. Sagarin (eds) *People in Places: The Sociology of the Familiar*. London: Nelson.
Savage, M., Bagnall, G. and Longhurst, B. (2005) *Globalization and Belonging*. London: Sage.
Sayer, A. (2005) *The Moral Significance of Class*. Cambridge: Cambridge University Press.
Schutz, A. (1964) 'The stranger: an essay in social psychology', in A. Schutz *Collected Papers: Vol.II*. The Hague: Martinus Nijhoff.
Schutz, A. and Luckmann, T. (1973) *The Structure of the Life World*. London: Heinemann.
Seabright, P. (2005) *The Company of Strangers: A Natural History of Economic Life*. Princeton, NJ: Princeton University Press.
Sen, A. (2006) *Identity and Violence: The Illusion of Destiny*. London: Allen Lane.
Sennett, R. (1974) *The Fall of Public Man*. New York: William Norton.
Seymour, D. and Sandiford, P. (2005) 'Learning emotion rules in service organizations: socialization and training in the UK public house sector', *Work, Employment and Society*, 19(3): 547–64.
Seymour, J. (2007) 'Treating the hotel like a home: the contribution of studying the single location home/workplace', *Sociology* 41(6): 1097–114.
Shorthose, J. (2004) 'Nottingham's *de facto* cultural quarter: the Lace Market, independents and a convivial ecology', in D. Bell and M. Jayne (eds) *City of Quarters: Urban Villages in the Contemporary City*. Aldershot: Ashgate.
Simmel, G. (1955) *Conflict and The Web of Group Affiliations*. Glencoe, IL: The Free Press.
Simmel, G. [1903] (1971) 'The metropolis and mental life', in G. Simmel *On Individuality and Social Forms: Selected Writings* (ed. D.N. Levine). Chicago: Chicago University Press.
Simmel, G. [1908] (1971) The stranger in G. Simmel *On Individuality and Social Forms: Selected Writings* (ed. D.N. Levine). Chicago: University of Chicago Press.
Smart, C. (2007) *Personal Life*. Cambridge: Polity.
Smith, A. [1759] (1976) *The Theory of Moral Sentiments*. Oxford: Clarendon Press.
Smith, N.D., Lister, M.R.A. and Middleton, S. (2005) 'Young people as active citizens: towards an inclusionary view of citizenship and constructing social participation', in J. Pilcher, C. Pole and J. Williams (eds) *Young People and Transitions: Becoming Citizens*. Basingstoke: Palgrave Macmillan.
Stokoe, E. (2006) 'Public intimacy in neighbour relationships and complaints', *Sociological Research Online*, 11(3).
Stone, A.R. (1994) 'Will the real body please stand up? Boundary stories about virtual cultures', in M. Benedikt (ed.) *Cyberspace: First Steps*. Cambridge, MA: MIT Press.

Strong, P. (1977) 'Medical errands: a discussion of routine patient work', in A. Davis and G. Horobin (eds) *Medical Encounters: The Experiences of Illness and Treatment*. London: Croom Helm.
Tadmor, N. (2001) *Family and Friends in Eighteenth-century England; Household, Kinship, Patronage*. Cambridge: Cambridge University Press.
Thompson, E.P. (1967) 'Time, work-discipline and industrial capitalism', *Past and Present*, 36: 57–97.
Topping, A. (2007) 'Career of tube voiceover woman hits buffers after online jokes misfire', *Guardian*, 27 November.
Toynbee, A.J. (1967) *Acquaintances*. London: Oxford University Press.
Trollope, A. [1880] (1995) *The Duke's Children*. Harmondsworth: Penguin.
Truss, L. (2006) *Talk to the Hand*. London: Profile Books.
Turkle, S. (1996) *Life on the Screen: Identity in an Age of the Internet*. London: Weidenfeld & Nicolson.
Vencat, E.F. (2007) 'Netting old friends', *Newsweek*, 15 January.
Vernon, P. (2006) 'Life as a gossip girl', *Observer Women*, July.
Vidich, A.J. and Bensman, J. (1958) *Small Town in Mass Society: Class, Power and Religion in a Rural Community*. New York: Doubleday Anchor Books.
Wadel, C. (1979) 'The hidden work of everyday life', in S. Wallman (ed.) *Social Anthropology of Work*. London: Academic Press.
Ward, L. (2007) 'Rich more neighbourly than poor, says study', *Guardian*, 18 October.
Washoff, F., Jamieson, L. and Smith, A. (2005) 'Solo living, individual and family boundaries: findings from secondary analysis', in L. McKie and S. Cunningham-Burley (eds) *Families in Society: Boundaries and Relationships*. Bristol: Policy Press.
Webb, B. and Stimson, G. (1976) 'Peoples' accounts of medical encounters', in M. Wadsworth and D. Robinson (eds) *Studies in Everyday Medical Life*. London: Martin Robertson.
Wenglinsky, M. (1973) 'Errands', in A. Birenbaum and E. Sagarin (eds) *People in Places: The Sociology of the Familiar*. London: Nelson.
Weinstein, D. and Weinstein, M.A. (1991) 'Georg Simmel: sociological bricoleur', *Theory, Culture and Society* 8(3): 151–68.
Werbner, P. (2008) 'Introduction: towards a new cosmopolitan anthropology', in P. Werbner (ed.) *Anthropology and the New Cosmopolitanism*. Oxford: Berg.
Westwood, S. (1985) *All Day, Every Day: Factory and Family in the Making of Women's Lives*. Urbana and Chicago: University of Illinois Press.
Wolff, K.H. (ed.) (1950) *The Sociology of Georg Simmel*. Glencoe, IL: The Free Press.
Wouters, C. (2001) 'The integration of classes and sexes in the twentieth century: etiquette books and emotion management', in T. Salumeti (ed.) *Norbert Elias and Human Interdependencies*. Montreal and Kingston: McGill-Queens University Press.
Wylie, I. (2006) 'Should employees encourage office relationships?', *Saturday Guardian: Work*, 14 January.
Zerubavel, E. (1981) *Hidden Rhythms: Schedules and Calendars in Social Life*. Chicago: Chicago University Press.
Zweig, F. (1961) *The Worker in an Affluent Society: Family Life and Industry*. London: Heinemann.

Name Index

Allan, G., 29
Argyle, K., 106
Ashby, M., 61

Bellow, S., 123
Bensman, J., 23
Benjamin, W., 85
Bergmann, J., 46, 111
Binnie, J., 123
Bishop, V., 49
Blokland, T., 1

Cavan, S., 71–2
Cavendish, R., 42, 43–4
Collinson, D., 42
Cooper, D., 74, 113
Coulthard, M., 61
Crow, G., 25, 29

Dalton, M., 46
Damer, S., 28
Davis, F., 82
Davis, M. S., 3–4, 7
Delanty, G., 69, 104–5, 116

Elias, N., 11, 12, 14, 119
Eyres, H., 47–8

Fairhurst, E., 63
Felski, R., 123–5
Finch, E., 92, 93
Firth, R., 63
Forseth, U., 79–80, 81
Fox, K., 37, 41, 47, 71, 75
Frankenberg, R., 18
Frisby, D., 11

Gans, H., 21, 22, 23–4, 27, 29, 97
Goffman, E., 2, 8, 10, 16, 19, 31, 32–3
Goldthorpe, J., 26–7, 37–8, 40
Granovetter, M., 9, 12–13, 115–16
Gustavsson, E., 102–3

Haavio-Mannila, E., 37
Hague, F., 111
Hamilton, P., 94–5
Hanley, L., 21, 30
Hannerz, U., 26, 27–8
Haugen, I., 21, 24, 25
Heath, C., 59
Hochschild, A., 50
Holtedahl, L., 21, 24, 25
Homans, G., 35
Hopper, E., 87
Hughes, E., 60
Hugman, R., 61

Jacobs, J., 24, 27, 87, 89
Jenkins, H., 100
Jonze, T., 104

Kamir, O., 92–3
Katz, F., 40
Keane, J., 120–1

Letherby, G., 70
Lewis, P., 44–5
Lofland, J., 81
Low, S., 85
Lury, C., 103

MacDonald, K., 56
Marshall, P., 98

Name Index

Melville, H., 83
Mills, C.W., 50
Moran, J., 69–70, 75
Morgan, D., 29–30, 31

Newcomb, T., 10

Oldenberg, R., 106, 117–18, 120

Pahl, R., 119
Perren, K., 23, 25
Pettinger, L., 47
Pevalin, D., 119

Rayner, J., 48
Richman, J., 82
Riesman, D., 115
Rojek, C., 92, 98
Roper, M., 46
Roy, D., 38–40
Reynolds, G., 70

Sanders, W., 72
Sandiford, P., 48–9
Sartre, J-P, 12
Savage, M., 26
Schutz, A., 3, 12
Sen, A., 123
Sennett, R., 96–7
Seymour, D., 48–9
Seymour, J., 84
Shields, R., 106

Shorthose, J., 89
Simmel, G., 3, 7–8, 9, 11, 13–14, 17, 88
Skeggs, B., 123
Smart, C., 61
Smith, A., 1, 6, 7, 12, 13, 35
Smith, N., 47
Stokoe, E., 22–3
Stone, A., 106
Strong, P., 54, 61

Topping, A., 102
Toynbee, A., 111–12
Trollope, A., 116–17
Truss, L., 122
Turkle, S., 103, 105–6

Vencat, E., 103–4
Vernon, P., 95
Vidich, A., 23

Wadel, C., 54, 80
Watson, J., 115
Ward, L., 26
Weinstein, D., 12
Weinstein, M., 12
Wenglinsky, M., 72
Westwood, S., 42–3, 44
Wouters, C., 119
Wylie, I., 37

Zerubavel, E., 68, 73
Zweig, F., 26, 37, 40

Subject Index

achievement and ascription, 108–9, 120, 122
aesthetic labour, 48, 80, 81
apartment blocks, 21, 30
autonomy
 at work, 41
 in professional practice, 58

boundaries, between acquaintances, strangers and intimates, 3, 7–9, 35, 108
bricolage, 12, 15
burnout, 58, 64

call centres, 49–51, 92, 102
caring, 57, 61
celebrations, 96–99
chat bots, 102–3
children, 25, 68, 113
churches, 73
civilizing process, 14
class, social, 20, 21, 22, 25–6, 28, 29, 42, 45–6, 78, 88–9, 116–17
client groups, 58
clock time, 67, 68
clubs, London, 78
communities, personal, 115–16
community, 18, 23, 29–30, 36, 40–1, 113, 117
conferences, 78
confidentiality, in professional-client relations, 60
contact, degree of, 16
conversation, 11, 22, 39, 71, 72, 110–11
consultations, professional, 57–60, 60–3
'convivial ecology', 89
cosmopolitanism, 123

cultural variations in idea of acquaintance-ship, 5, 62
cyberbullying, 105

Dick Barton (radio series), 99–100,
dinner parties, 78
distance and closeness, 11–12, 19, 21, 26, 28, 33–4, 40, 48, 50, 71, 74, 81, 108
 in professional-client relations, 53, 60–2, 64

email, 102
embodiment and disembodiment, 49–51, 92, 101–7
emotional labour, 48–9, 61, 80, 81
emotions, 37, 45
Englishness, 71, 75, 81
errands, 54, 72–3, 125
ethics of acquaintanceship, 121–3
 see also distance and closeness, etiquette
ethics of space, 33–4
ethnicity, 20, 21, 39, 43, 45
etiquette, 5, 32, 70, 71, 80, 113, 122
everyday life, 34, 52, 76, 123–5

fictional characters as acquaintances, 99–101, 107
flaneurs, 85
flexibility at work, 46–7
formal and informal systems at work, 35–6
friends, 6, 7, 9, 36, 36–8, 42–3, 104, 113, 116, 119

gender, 25, 39, 41–5, 57, 74–5, 80, 101, 116, 116–18, 124
globalization, 84, 117

Subject Index

gossip, 22, 45–6, 90, 111, 115
gossip columnists, 95–6
'great, good places', 106

habit, 125
hidden work, 80
history, of acquaintanceship, 13, 16, 468, 118–19
home, 124

interchangeability, lack of in acquaintanceship, 5
and strangers, 87
internet, the, 92, 102–7, 107, 119
intimacy, 1, 2, 4, 6, 7, 8, 12, 13, 18, 19, 20, 37, 96, 110, 121, 122, 125
dimensions, of, 2–3
in professional practice, 53
public, 22–3

jokes, joking, 41, 42, 43, 44, 51

knowledge, 9–11, 11, 16, 18, 22, 23, 31, 38, 40, 64, 67, 74, 75, 108, 126
and celebrities, 97–8
and fleeting acquaintances, 82–4, 90
guilty, 60
in professional-client relations, 53–4, 59–60, 63
and stalking, 93–4
and unwanted encounters, 94–5
'knowership', 8

late modernity, 109, 118–19
leisure activities, 73
life-course, 20, 21, 25, 43, 45, 113–14

masculinity, 39, 42, 43, 57, 71, 75
mates, 36–8, 42
metropolis, 7, 8, 14
see also urban life
mobility, 119
MUDs ('multi-user domains'), 106

names, 11
name-dropping, 111, 114
neighbourhoods, 18, 19, 20, 21, 24, 27–30, 124
sub-divisions within, 27–8
neighbouring, 19, 20–6, 24
neighbours, 4
defined, 19

networking, 51–2, 111–12,
networks, social, 1, 12, 32, 76, 115–16, 118
nicknames, 41, 42, 71, 74
'Nighthawks' (painting), 87
night-time economy, 86
noise, 23, 28

objectivity,
in professional-client relations, 57–8
one-off encounters, 83
ontological security, 34, 69, 116

para-social relations, 97
Parque Central (San Jose), 85
pinball machines, 72
pockets, 26
post-offices, 113, 121
power differentials and acquaintanceship, 60, 61
practices of acquaintanceship, 109–12
professional ethics, 56
professional gaze, the, 58
professionalization, 56
'prosthetic culture', 103
public and private distinction, 24, 98, 112–13, 120, 120–1
pubs, 71–2, 75–6, 106
'pure sociability', 9, 11, 71, 88

reciprocity, 23–4, 90, 108
lack of in distant and unwanted encounters, 91–2, 93–4, 95–6, 96–101, 101
lack of in professional-client relations, 53, 57, 64
recognition, 121
regulars, 70–2, 75–6
'relationality', 61
rituals, 43, 47
'rough and respectable' distinction, 28, 29
rules, and fleeting acquaintances, 78–82

segmentation of relationships, 40–1
self, the, 12, 101, 114
'seriality', 12, 124, 125
service economy, 47–9, 80, 81, 83, 84, 86, 87–8, 89, 90, 119
shared residences, 30–1
Sherlock Holmes, 99
sites of acquaintanceship, 112–13
sociologists and acquaintanceship, 125–6
space, social, 1

'Speakers' Corner' (Hyde Park, London), 74, 86, 113
stalking, 92–4, 98, 107
'Star Trek', 100
stories, 29–30, 62, 74, 82, 114–15
strangers, 1, 2, 3, 4, 5, 6, 7, 8, 13, 14, 18, 27, 73–4, 77, 79, 85, 87, 90
 known strangers, 3, 9, 18, 20, 66

taxi drivers, 82
'timescapes', 67–8

total institutions, 19, 31–3
tourism, 84, 86
trains, 65–6, 69–70, 75
'trato', 47–8,
trial and error in neighbouring, 21

urban life, 18, 67, 77, 82–3, 84–5, 86–7, 89, 119, 125
urban myths, 114–15

weak ties, 9, 12–13, 76, 114, 115–16, 117

Related books from Open University Press
Purchase from www.openup.co.uk or order through your local bookseller

COMMUNITY
WELFARE, CRIME AND SOCIETY
Gerry Mooney and Sarah Neal (eds)

This text provides an excellent basis for engaging students with the issues surrounding both the idea of 'community' in relation to social policy and the complex processes of policy formation and implementation with a 'community' dimension. Essentially it offers a practical critique based on a combination of a clear, intellectual engagement and well developed illustration. A particular strength is the inclusion of material which gets beyond the immediate context of the UK and draws on examples from colonial and post-colonial practice in the management of 'problem populations'. The book will be of great value to both undergraduate students across the social sciences and to students undertaking professional programmes in social work, community work and related fields.
Professor David Byrne, School of Applied Social Sciences,
University of Durham, UK

The concept of community is among the most contested of social science ideas. At the heart of this book is an examination of the concept's unique ability to represent the notion of collective well-being and positive social relations and to denote a description or categorisation of social problems and 'problem populations'.

This paradox makes the idea of community particularly valuable for understanding the diverse and complex ways in which social welfare and crime control policies affect each other.

The chapters are organised to make sense of community in a range of ways: as a theoretical, political and populist discourse; as a vehicle for policy interventions; as an instrument of social governance and social ordering; and as a basis of collective action.

The book considers community within historical and contemporary contexts, in the UK and internationally. It highlights many of the key social science debates as well as adiverse range of early 21st century policy agendas and social issues, such as social cohesion, community safety and anti-social behaviour.

Each chapter highlights issues of evidence and the role that different forms of social data play in the analysis of ideas of community and communities.

Community is a key text for students on social policy, sociology, criminology and general social sciences courses.

Contributors: John Clarke, Allan Cochrane, Gordon Hughes, Gerry Mooney, Sarah Neal, Janet Newman, Sharon Pinkney and Esther Saraga.

Contents: Notes on contributors – Series preface – Community: themes and debates – Community and policymaking – Community, social change and social order – Community safety and the governance of 'problem populations' – Communities and social mobilisations – Conclusion – Acknowledgements – Index.

2008   208pp
978–0–335–22934–5 (Paperback)   978–0–335–22933–8 (Hardback)

YOUNG PEOPLE AND SOCIAL CHANGE 2/E
NEW PERSPECTIVES
Andy Furlong and Fred Cartmel

Reviews of the first edition:

Not only does the clarity of the authors' writing make the book very accessible, but their argument is also illustrated throughout with a broad range of empirical material ... undoubtedly a strong contribution to the study of both contemporary youth and 'late-modern' society.
Youth Justice

A very accessible, well-evidenced and important book. ... It succeeds in raising important questions in a new and powerful way.
Journal of Education and Work

the book will be very popular with students and with academics. ... The clarity of the organization, expression and argument is particularly commendable. I have no doubt that *Young People and Social Change* will rightly find its way onto the recommended reading lists of many in the field.
Professor Robert MacDonald, University of Teesside

A welcome update to one of the most influential and authoritative books on young people in modern societies. With a fuller theoretical explanation and drawing on a comprehensive range of studies from Europe, North America, Australia and Japan, the second edition of *Young People and Social Change* is a valuable contribution to the field. The authors examine modern theoretical interpretations of social change in relation to young people and provide an overview of their experiences in a number of key contexts such as education, employment, the family, leisure, health, crime and politics.

Building on the success of the previous edition, the second edition offers an expanded theoretical approach and wider coverage of empirical data to take into account worldwide developments in the field. Drawing on a wealth of research evidence, the book highlights key differences between the experiences of young people in different countries in the developed world.

Young People and Social Change offers a wide-ranging and up-to-date introductory text for students in sociology of youth, sociology of education, social stratification and related fields.

Contents
List of figures – The authors – Acknowledgements – Series editor's preface – The risk society – Change and continuity in education – Social change and labour market transitions – Changing patterns of dependency – Leisure and lifestyles – Health risks in late modernity – Crime and insecurity – Politics and participation – The epistemological fallacy of late modernity – Notes – References – Index.

2006   208pp
978–0–335–21868–4 (Paperback)   978–0–335–21869–1 (Hardback)

CULTURAL CHANGE AND ORDINARY LIFE
Brian Longhurst

- How important are the media?
- How is culture changing?
- How is ordinary life being transformed?
- How do we belong?

This ground-breaking book offers a new approach to the understanding of everyday life, the media and cultural change. It explores the social pattern of ordinary life in the context of recent theories and accounts of social and cultural change.

Brian Longhurst argues that our social and cultural lives are becoming increasingly audienced and performed and that activities in everyday life are changing due to the ever-growing importance and salience of the media. These changes involve people forging new ways of belonging, where among other things they seek to distinguish themselves from others.

In *Cultural Change and Ordinary Life*, Longhurst evaluates changes in the media and ordinary life in the context of large-scale cultural change, especially with respect to globalization and hybridisation, fragmentation, spectacle and performance, and enthusing or fan-like activities. He makes the case that analysis of the media has to be brought into a more thorough dialogue with other forms of research that have looked at social processes.

Cultural Change and Ordinary Life is key reading for students and researchers of sociology, media studies, cultural studies and mass communication.

Contents
Acknowledgements – Introduction – Concepts and theories of everyday and ordinary life – Changing ordinary life – Understanding and theorizing cultural change – Globalizing, hybridizing and localizing: processes of elective belonging – Imagining, performing and identifying: class, identity and culture – Distinguishing and connecting 1: capitals and the use of time – Distinguishing and connecting 2: the omnivore thesis – Enthusing – Conclusions – References – Index.

2007   192pp
978–0–335–22187–5 (Paperback)   978–0–335–22188–2 (Hardback)